Secrets to Spiritual Success

Success

Paul Estabrooks

Sovereign World

Sovereign World Ltd
PO Box 777
Tonbridge
Kent TN11 9XT
England

Scripture quotations are taken from the Holy Bible, New International Version. Copyright © 1973, 1978, 1984 by International Bible Society Used by permission.

ISBN: 1 85240 190 7

Typeset by CRB Associates, Lenwade, Norwich.
Printed in England by Clays Ltd, St. Ives plc.

to Mom and Dad...
who taught me these secrets
since childhood

Contents

Foreword

Without conversations and communication there would be no relationships. Two-thousand-year-old examples are found at the end of several epistles, written by some of the apostles.

They write about Timothy – in Christ my son, or Gaius – my host, or touchingly, the mother of Rufus, who is also *my* mother.

What do you think of Priscilla and Aquila *'my fellow workers in Christ Jesus, who risked their necks for my life'*!

Pretty exciting – and I could make this list longer; long from Scripture and very long if I could go through all of history church history, that is. Exciting because all these relationships were *new* ones and they all existed solely on the basis of someone having come into their lives: the Lord Jesus Christ. They are, so to speak, illustrations to prove the reality of the Gospel, proofs of their beliefs. I wish I had more expressions to say what I mean, but I hope you understand me.

And that is what my friend, brother and colleague Paul Estabrooks has done in this book which I strongly recommend. Not sermonizing, but introducing. The moment you read one of these stories, your life is enriched. You then have a new relationship with a real person, made real on these pages.

A person who is not only interesting and as part of your family long overdue to be introduced to you. No, it is more. It is often a person who has paid a price for his or her faith. Who has become an example and an inspiration; part of what the Bible calls a *'cloud of witnesses'*. Without them we would not make it.

You'll be a richer person after you have met them in this book. And you can become as spiritually successful as they.

Brother Andrew

Success is neither fame, wealth, nor power...

Charles Malik

> 'The secret of the Lord is with those who fear Him...'[1] (Psalm 25:14)

Introduction

Significant Secrets

Ceiling fans whirl overhead to move the heavy, tepid air. The large circular sanctuary is filled with quiet worshippers as the piano strikes the first musical note of a hymn. The song leader sings out softly over the PA system, 'I can hear my Saviour calling ... I can hear my Saviour calling...' The attentive congregation intone each line in response. You sense they really mean what they are singing.

The leader concludes...

'Where He leads me I will follow.
Where He leads me I will follow.
Where He leads me I will follow.
I'll go with Him ... with Him ...
all the way.'

The packed room swells with harmonious singing as newer and younger worshippers grasp the tune and lyrics. Soon the worship center is filled with musical expression of total commitment and discipleship to Jesus Christ.

This is not a description of a North American church experience but a group of worshippers in Beijing, China on Sunday, July 25, 1993. And of course, they are singing in the Chinese language.

People sit in the congregation who have paid a high price to follow Jesus. Some have spent years in prison. Some have lost family members to earlier persecution. Most know what it really means to sacrifice for Jesus.

In spite of the oppressive heat, they hang on every word of the service with intensity. Many are rapidly taking notes of the morning message from a pastor who spent fifteen years in prison for his faith. The sermon text is Luke 7:36–38 – the sinful woman who washed Jesus' feet with her tears and dried them with her hair.

Our young Chinese guide is gripped by the message of forgiveness. Following the service she kneels and asks Jesus for the forgiveness she realizes she needs. She commits her life to him as Lord and Saviour. Later she writes in a letter ... 'I told my parents and colleagues about Jesus Christ ... I am thankful for all His help and He is my best friend now. I am glad you led me to Him.'

Later on that same day an elderly Chinese house-church pastor and his wife share their life story. He has spent twenty-one years and eight months of his ministry years in prison. Yet with a smile he says, **'That was nothing compared to what Jesus suffered on the cross for me!'**

His tiny wife of more than fifty years sits beaming at his side. She shares the difficulties of life with six children and a mother-in-law to feed when her husband was gone for so long. She concludes, **'It is good when our children experience hardships because then they learn for themselves that God is faithful!'**

In the same room is a tall, young professional basketball player. He has been a believer in Jesus for only two years. Wistfully he shares his plan to quit basketball at the end of the year to become an itinerant evangelist in the countryside. His fiancee at his side is still weighing the cost of this future plan before final commitment to a marriage.

As the day concludes, the group of North Americans with whom I am travelling evaluate our impressions. We ponder why folk back home don't exude this same commitment, joy and simplicity of faith. For days we discuss these weighty issues. And we conclude that there really is such a thing as spiritual success. But in our countries it is the best kept secret in the world!

Devotional writer Oswald Chambers, says the sign of friendship is not when a friend tells you his or her secret sorrows,

'... but the final mark of intimacy is when [friends] share their secret joys with you. Have we ever let God tell us any of His joys? ... Are we so intimately united to Jesus Christ's idea of prayer – *"Your will be done"* (Matthew 6:10) – **that we catch the secrets of God?'** [2] (emphasis added)

For the past seventeen years that I have been involved in ministry to the Suffering Church through Open Doors, I have researched the essence of this spiritual success. I have listened to secret joys as well as secret sorrows. More importantly, I have watched how these worked out in daily life when the 'small' blessings from God revealed his amazing intimacy in individual lives.

Although there is significant crossover among the lessons, principles and illustrations, in this volume I have narrowed them down to seven 'big ideas' or major principles which are succinctly stated at the beginning of each chapter and collated together at the end of the book.

My utilization of the term 'Suffering Church' refers to our brothers and sisters who live under external restrictions – limited in some way in the practising or the sharing of their faith in Christ.

But I quickly hasten to add that these **secrets** or principles describe a spirituality that is consistent with the pages of the Bible and the heart of God. They cannot be written off as just cultural differences. Each secret with its many sub-sections is very much biblically based and forms what one of my favourite authors, Watchman Nee, refers to as the **normal** Christian life. Others may rightly conclude that the secrets are a call to simplicity, to get 'back to basics' ... to meat and potatoes faith.

Two assumptions: first, the challenging testimonies from members of the Suffering Church do not imply that every member was or is always victorious nor constantly living in all these secrets. They too are human beings with as many frailties as we. There are many failure stories as well as the many success stories. Some of these will be shared in appropriate chapters.

Secondly, these secrets shared from the lives of believers from mostly the two-thirds world – or creative-access countries – are not designed to lay a guilt trip on Christians in the West. Even Jesus' closest disciples asked him to show them the father, not realizing that God most often exhibits himself in his children rather than to his children.

It is hoped that the reality of spiritual success in the lives of Suffering Church members will challenge us to truly evaluate our own infections of rationalism, materialism and sophistication and show us the source of true spiritual vitality.

My prayer is that these principles will no longer be secrets in our understanding and will therefore be applied in a very practical way to our daily living. Then you too can be a spiritual success!

*To love the Lord your God
is the heartbeat of our mission.*

Jon Mohr and Randall Dennis

Secret One –
Wholehearted love for God

What our good and loving God wants
most from you and me is our undivided
love for him – above all else – proven in
obedience to him and love for all others
... and rewarded with his goodness and
fatherly caring.

Chapter 1

Lovers for Life

Her eyes flash joyfully on a soft face with lines etched by years of cares. It is six weeks after the infamous Tiananmen Square massacre and we are sitting at her feet in a hotel room in Beijing, China. Affectionately known as 'Auntie Esther', this diminutive elderly Chinese medical doctor keeps us spell bound with her personal testimony of God's faithfulness. Her soft, kind voice masks the many years of suffering through which she has passed.

'During the cultural revolution,' she continues, 'I was called in by my superior one day. At that time I was in charge of eight large pediatric wards in my hospital.

'The communists were cracking down on people who did not toe the current party line. My superior warned me that I should deny my faith and join the communist party or I may have to face the serious consequences of job demotion and salary reduction.

'A few days later, I was rudely awakened by four nurses who roughly pulled me from my bed and marched me to the hospital. En route they stopped at a barber shop and shaved off half of my hair. In front of the rest of the staff, I was confronted to renounce my faith in Christ and join the communist party.

'I responded, "I can't deny Jesus. I love Jesus!" At the mention of his name they threw me down on the ground and cursed. Later, the communist cadre at my hospital tore the stethoscope from my neck and said, "You are no longer Esther; you are now The Fool".'

We sit in tears as we try to envisage experiences like these which we have only heard about but never had to live out.

Esther continues. For the next eleven years she lived in the basement of the hospital and obediently submitted to her new task – cleaning the floors and toilets of the hospital wards which she previously headed. Her already meagre salary of 50 Yuan per month was reduced to 15 Yuan.[1] And she had to buy the cleaning materials from it. The rest was used up on food.

But Esther practised the presence of Jesus in her job. She sang as she toiled. With a twinkle in her eyes she adds, 'My hospital had the cleanest floors and cleanest toilets in all of China!'

Hospital staff would come to her and with great envy question her source of joy in spite of her troubles. Esther responded, **'When you have Jesus in your heart, it doesn't matter what job you do or what position you have. It only matters that you love him and are faithful and loyal to him!'**

When the cultural revolution period ended, Aunty Esther was reinstated in her original job and given back-pay for all that she had been deprived of during those eleven years. This enabled her to send one of her children to the USA for higher education.

Aunty Esther is only one of many lives from the Suffering Church that have quietly communicated the simple but deeply profound message that what God asks of us – above all else – is our wholehearted love for him. Everything and everyone else is to pale in importance to our passionate devotion to him alone. A contemporary calls it 'head-over-heels, white-hot' love for God.[2]

And this devotion is totally personal. Something quite different from mere religious devotion – devotion to principles or causes. Love not defined as a sentimental emotion, but rather a deliberate act of my will.

Jesus declared God-love the essence of all God required of mankind throughout biblical history. He summed up the law and the prophets with a reference to Deuteronomy 6:5:

> *'Love the Lord your God with all your heart and with all your soul and with all your strength.'*

Jesus thus declared love for God as the *first* and *greatest* commandment. And the flip side of the coin is to love your neighbour as yourself[3] – the outward evidence of the inner reality of truly loving God. Love that is 'selfless' as opposed to 'selfish'. These two love directives then are the summation of all the commandments of God.

The tropical island of Cuba has a very unique tree called the agueye. It is different in that it has two sets of roots. There is the main unseen inner root from which the tree draws its life. There are also other roots which are visible and decorative, hanging from the tree's branches. Wholehearted love for God is to be our sustenance and main-rooted source of life. Love for others is often the outward visible, 'decorative' evidence of that inner commitment to God.

Throughout the Scriptures are reminders that whatever we do for God, we are to do *wholeheartedly*. The imagery is also of one who is singleminded and not one with a double mind.

Caleb was noted in the Old Testament as a man with whom God was especially pleased. He was singled out to see and then live in the promised land. Not only because he joined Joshua in giving a good report about the land they spied out, but because he had 'a different spirit' and followed after God whole-heartedly.[4]

The world may elevate the quality of being 'cool' but God wants his followers to be 'hot'. In fact, he says that those who are 'cool' (neither hot nor cold) he expels like vomit.[5]

Intimate Friends

'She was only nineteen at the time when her crumpled body was roughly thrown into the dungeon cell. There was no light. All she knew was that it was somewhere underground. The floor was all wet. The smell told her it was human excrement. Rats and vermin were everywhere. There was no bed, so if she was to get any rest, it would be sitting in her own waste and that of others before her. As she sat on the floor, she felt something warm run down her arm. She grabbed it and for the first time realized she was still bleeding from the beating.

Her body began to swell from the beating. Silently, squatting so as little of her body as possible would rest on the floor, she began to thank the Lord she was worthy to suffer for him. All she would have to do was denounce her Saviour, but she refused, and here she was – alone, beaten and weeping tears of joy as her cell became her house of peace. Quietly she asked him for wisdom and strength, not that she would get out of this terrible place, but that wherever he put her, she would be able to continue to preach the gospel of her Lord.'[6]

This story of Mrs Chen in China is graphically described by my good friend, Carl Lawrence, in his moving book *The Church In China*. The first time I heard Mrs Chen share this testimony, she added, 'In the prison I came to the point where I told Jesus I loved him just for himself, not for what he could do for me nor for what I could get from him.'

Jesus Christ desires us to walk with him in a relationship of special intimacy. He says,

> *'I no longer call you servants, because a servant does not know his master's business. Instead I have called you friends, for everything that I learned from my Father I have made known to you.'*[7]

His own self-sacrifice and his total communication of the Father warrants and demands our total love and commitment to him.

Unfortunately, our western cultural mindset has often conditioned us to love someone – especially God – for what we can get out of the relationship rather than for what we can give to it. Oswald Chambers reminds us:

> 'God wants you in a closer relationship to Himself than receiving His gifts. He wants you to get to know Him ... My goal is God Himself, not joy nor peace, nor even blessing, but Himself, my God.'[8]

One of China's most loved pastors, Wang Ming-dao, spent a total of more than twenty-three years in prison. When finally released, he referred to the experience as 'my honeymoon with Jesus.' During a visit from Open Doors co-workers, he was asked if he had any prayer requests. He replied, **'Pray for us that we will love the Lord more!'**

Worldteam missionaries tell of a Cuban pastor in the early 1960s who was told by a local policeman exulting in his new faith in marxism, 'We can wipe out the church in Cuba!'

The pastor replied, 'Yes, you can destroy all the church buildings in Cuba, but I have Jesus Christ in my heart and you can never take him away from me!'

In Russia, pastor Peter Peters suffered over eleven years of appalling conditions in the gulags of Siberia, including lengthy periods of solitary confinement. When asked what sustained him he replied, 'The presence of Jesus.'

Centuries ago Thomas à Kempis had grasped this concept and penned the following in *The Imitation Of Christ*.

'Happiness comes to the person who knows how to love Jesus and to disregard himself for Christ's sake. Our love for Jesus must exceed all other loves. Love the world and you will collapse when it collapses; embrace Jesus and you will have stability forever.

Love him. Keep him as a friend. When all others forsake you, he will remain faithful to the end.

Eventually, whether you choose it or not, you will be separated from everyone else. Therefore, stay close to Jesus in both life and death. Trust his fidelity. When all others fail, he alone can help you.

It is your Beloved's nature to desire no rivals, to ask for your full devotion.

If you look to Jesus in all things, you will certainly find him. And if you look only for yourself, you will find only yourself, but it will be your loss. Those who do not seek Jesus bring more harm on themselves than all their enemies could ever inflict.'[9]

More than Family

Pastor Mikhail Khorev spent many years in the Soviet Gulag and wrote a series of letters to his family over those years. In his fourth letter, he shared an incident from his youth that had great impact:

> 'When father was arrested he suggested that we pray together as a family before he left. I can no longer remember what I prayed or what my mother and sisters prayed, but I do remember what my father prayed: "Dear Lord, I love my wife and children very much. But more than anything else in the world, Lord, I love you and this is why I have chosen the narrow way of thorns. I commend my family to you, O Lord, with all their needs and requirements, and I am comforted that you always remain faithful to your promises. I know that in the days to come I will see my whole family again before your throne ... "
>
> My dear children, that day I thanked the Lord especially for my parents, who had loved God with all their hearts, minds and souls.' [10]

Mikhail often wrote to his family of his great love for them but also of his greater love for Jesus. In one of his quoted prayers he expressed it this way,

> 'It might be difficult for my children at times, and my loved ones might have reproaches hurled at them sometimes, but nevertheless I love you, Lord, more than anything else, and that is why I have left family to consecrate myself to your service.' [11]

The most difficult saying of our Lord is the injunction that to truly love him and serve him we must hate our father, mother, siblings, spouse and children. Taken at a surface level interpretation, this command seems to conflict with Jesus' instructions to love everyone.

Most Bible scholars are convinced that Jesus is simply making a very strong statement that our love for him is to be challenged by no other – even those whom we hold most dear, our own family.

Even the patriarch Abraham, who waited so long for a son and heir, was tested by God in this area. God wanted to know if Abraham loved him more than his much-loved son, Isaac. And so the command to sacrifice. Yet in this act of Abraham's submission, God revealed his own love in preparing a substitute – a foreshadowing of his own son, the ultimate sacrifice.

Dr Paul Negrut pastored the largest Baptist church in Europe which is located in Oradea, Romania. He served the church faithfully under the cruel Ceaucescu regime and often suffered personal mistreatment.

He shared with our Open Doors leaders that the most difficult time he remembers was a night he returned home rejoicing after a very successful evangelistic crusade. But when he walked in the house, he saw his wife weeping and his nine-year-old daughter was trembling. Through her tears his wife shared that when their daughter was coming home from school that day, the Securitate (Romanian secret police) tried to rape her to destroy her and the family.

Paul said,

> 'That night I was in a great struggle. For the first time I was thinking to emigrate from Romania. I asked the Lord, "Should I leave the blessing of suffering or should I endure to see my girl like that?"
>
> 'I talked to my wife and we chose to stay. Two days later they tried to rape her again. And two days later they tried to rape my wife. But every time God was protecting them in a miraculous way.' [12]

The suffering of family members is probably the most difficult persecution to endure. But when we focus on our love for God even above family, God honours that decision and often binds the family members even closer together.

One wise elderly pastor in China told our couriers who were a happily married couple, 'You must love God more than you love each other, and that will strengthen your marriage.'

Chinese Pastor Wang Ming-dao was under tremendous pressure after his first arrest. He was promised release from prison and the return to his pulpit if he would just 'preach for the government'. In his mind this would be lying and he was certain he could not live a hypocritical life.

Pastor Wang was firm in his resolve, until he heard that his beloved wife Debra had also been arrested and was in grave danger. He heard that she was not eating properly and was growing critically weak because of the poor food she was receiving in prison. She would not survive if something were not done. This news so disturbed him that he broke and agreed with his persecutors that he would preach 'a lie' and join the government-controlled church.

His plan was to get his wife to safety with her mother and then he would commit suicide. He reportedly wandered the streets murmuring, 'I am Peter ... I am Peter ...' and his heart-sickness began to affect his body.

When the authorities realized that he would not compromise himself by preaching in the government-controlled church, Pastor Wang and Debra were re-arrested. She received a fifteen year sentence and he life imprisonment.

Early in this second imprisonment, God brought to his mind the verses Micah 7:7–9, which he had memorized at the age of twenty-one:

> *'But as for me, I keep watch for the Lord, I wait in hope for God my Saviour; my God will hear me. Do not gloat over me, my enemy! Though I have fallen, I will rise. Though I sit in darkness, the Lord will be my light. Because I have sinned against him, I will bear the Lord's wrath, until he pleads my case and establishes my right. He will bring me out into the light; I will see his justice.'*

Wang Ming-dao was no longer afraid – for himself or his wife. He was finally released in 1980 at eighty years of age – very frail, nearly blind and all-but-deaf. He had served over twenty-three years in prison. His wife Debra had been released three years earlier for health reasons. For the remaining eleven years of his life he was a great encouragement to the church in China as well as to the many foreign visitors he and Debra entertained.[13]

The Philippines is a country you would not expect to hear of persecution in Christian families. But the southern island of Mindanao is dominantly Muslim.

Comba Banda is a former Muslim whose father was an imam – a Muslim priest. He was a notorious gang leader and spent years in prison for robbery and murder. But there in prison he met Jesus Christ.

After his release, he was so effective in leading Muslims to Jesus back home in Mindanao that Muslim fundamentalists in his area kidnapped his fourteen-year-old daughter, Esterlita, in late 1991. They would only return her if he recanted his faith and return to Islam. He and his wife prayed intensely about this and felt they could not give in to this blackmail. He continued to preach for three years with no definite news about his little girl.

He concludes,

'Despite the terrible things they have done to my daughter, I fear no one but God alone! Pray for my daughter **and that I will continue to preach Christ**.'[14] (emphasis added)

We may say how heartless this response is for the family. Who provides and cares for them? In early 1995, Comba Banda received a message from Esterlita. She shared with her father that she had been sold into prostitution in neighbouring East Malaysia. But God had helped her escape. She was then taken in by a sympathetic Malaysian family and hidden for her safety. And now she has fallen in love with a young man and married him. They hope to visit Comba Banda in a safe place in the near future.

All through the Scriptures, God also repeats his love and concern for the widows and fatherless. Mrs Chen in China was an effective itinerant evangelist. Her husband, a mathematics teacher, was interned in a labour camp and her eldest son Peter, a young teenager, was martyred by the Red Guards during the infamous cultural revolution.

She was thus left alone to care for the three remaining young children, all under ten years of age. Yet she continually put herself at risk because she loved God above all else. And God commanded her to continue her evangelistic preaching tours. Here's how she described to me one incident of God's provision for the family:

'One day I said to my children, "The Lord has told me that today I will go to prison for Him. Father is not at home so please behave. Love each other and don't forget to bring food for your mom!"

During that time there were so many prisoners that the government could not provide for all of them so family members provided their food.

The children cried when they heard this. Daniel retorted, "But mom, we have only five catties of rice left. How can we have rice and also send you some? When it's all gone, we'll die!"

I told the children, "The Lord can turn nothing into something!" and I reminded them of the story of Elijah and the widow. They had a simple child-like faith and believed that God could provide for their need.

So they concluded, "Even though our rice is not enough, we will cook for you too!"

After talking with the children, The Public Security Bureau personnel came to the door and arrested me. Daniel followed me to the prison to find out which cell I would be in. The younger two children knelt in prayer. As I was taken away, my heart was wrenched as I heard their little voices trailing off.

I was in prison on that occasion for thirty days. All the while Daniel faithfully sent rice for me. When I returned home I asked, "Is there any rice left?"

Daniel's response was, "Mom, our rice container is over-flowing!" It really was. Those five catties had inexplicably grown to about forty catties and was literally overflowing the container.

I said, "Praise the Lord! Now we can cook for the other inmates and feed them as well." The Lord's grace is beyond measure.'[15]

But it works the other way with parents also. I remember so well a moving interview with Jennifer, a young university student in central China. She had come to Christ through a foreign English teacher's influence. This was just after the infamous Tiananmen Square massacre.

Jennifer went home one weekend after her conversion to share with her parents her joy in finding Christ. But to her amazement her parents reacted with violence. Her father physically beat her and told her to get out of the house if she was going to follow this 'foreign religion'. As she collected her things and prepared to leave, her mother stood weeping at the doorway imploring her to give up her faith and stay home.

In a state of physical shock and emotional confusion, Jennifer returned to her dormitory room wondering what to do. She went to her Bible and it fell open at Psalm 27. She was amazed when she came to verse 10:

'Though my father and mother forsake me, the Lord will receive me.'

In her commitment to Jesus, she received strength to carry on even in face of the opposition from her parents whom she loved. She now reports a softening attitude at home because of her loving spirit.

My colleague Dr John Pitt, shares the poignant story of a young Christian in Egypt he met named Timothy. Through Christian radio broadcasts Timothy was introduced to Jesus whom he received into his heart and began to follow.

But when he shared his new faith with his Muslim family, they reacted so strongly that he was told to leave home and never come back. After several years of living with other Christians, he decided to try and make contact with his family again. On his mother's birthday, he bought some flowers and walked to his family's home. When he knocked on the door, his mother opened it.

'Happy birthday, Mother,' Timothy said, 'I brought you these flowers because I love you!'

Timothy's mother turned to him with a stern look and said, 'I don't know who you are!' And she slammed the door.

Timothy said to John with tears streaming down his face, 'I don't have a family any more. Will you be my family?'

Jesus said to his disciples,

> '... *no one who has left home or wife or brothers or parents or children for the sake of the kingdom of God will fail to receive many times as much in this age and, in the age to come, eternal life.*'[16]

Obey Commands

Romanian pastor Dr Paul Negrut was visiting an old friend in Romania named Trian Dors in his humble home. As Paul entered, he realized that Trian was bleeding from open wounds. He asked, 'What happened?'

Trian replied, 'The secret police have just left my home. They came and confiscated my manuscripts. Then they beat me.'

Paul says, 'I began to complain about the heavy tactics of the secret police. But Trian stopped me saying, "Brother Paul, it is so sweet to suffer for Jesus. God didn't bring us together tonight to complain but to praise him. Let's kneel down and pray."

'He knelt and began praying for the secret police. He asked God to bless them and save them. He told God how much he loved them. He said, "God, if they will come back in the next few days, I pray that you will prepare me to minister to them."'

Paul continued, 'By this time I was ashamed. I thought I had been living the most difficult life in Romania for the Lord. And I was bitter about that.'

Trian Dors then shared with Paul how the secret police had been coming to his home regularly for several years. They beat him twice every week. They confiscated all his papers. After the beating he would talk to the officer in charge. Trian would look into his eyes and say, 'Mister, I love you. And I want you to know that if our next meeting is before the judgement throne of God, you will not go to hell because I hate you but because you rejected love.' Trian would repeat these words after every beating.

Years later that officer came alone to his home one night. Trian prepared himself for another beating. But the officer spoke kindly and said, 'Mr Dors, the next time we meet will be before the judgement throne of God. I came tonight to apologize for what I did to you and to tell you that your love moved my heart. I have asked Christ to save me. But two days ago the doctor discovered that I have a very severe case of cancer and I have only a few weeks to live before I go to be with God. I came tonight to tell you that we will be together on the other side.'[17]

One of my favourite authors, Charles Colson, wrote an entire book on the subject of loving God because he sensed that most professing Christians really don't know how to love God. He wrote,

> 'If we would love God we must love His justice and act upon it. Then taking a holy, radical stand – contra mundum if need be – we surrender the illusion of power and find it replaced by True Power.'[18]

No sooner do we wilfully decide to love the Lord with all our being than we hear Jesus' words, *'If you love me, you will obey what I command.'*[19] And one of his most difficult commands is to love even our enemies.

Mrs Chen from China was in prison three times. Afterwards she concluded, 'There is only one way to respond to torture and interrogation. That way is God's love.' Then she added, 'When you meet their cruelty with the love of Jesus, they often run out of words. It will even lead them to seek Jesus for themselves.'[20]

Armando Valladares shares a similar testimony. He spent twenty-two years in Fidel Castro's terrible prison system in Cuba. He was finally released after much political pressure. His wife lobbied for him from other countries. Shortly after his release, he shared about his lowest moments in a *TIME* magazine interview:

> 'That period was one of the worst. But I felt myself neither alone nor abandoned because God was with me inside that jail. The greater the hatred my jailers directed at me, the more my heart brimmed over with Christian love and faith. I never felt hatred for my jailers, and even today, with the detachment of time, I offer prayers for them that they might repent.' [21]

In his moving prison autobiography *Against All Hope*, Valladares shares about a Christian fellow prisoner who impacted him deeply, especially whenever they were being mistreated.

> 'Suddenly one prisoner, as the guards rained blows on his back, raised his arms and face to the sky and shouted, "Forgive them, Lord, for they know not what they do!" There was no trace of pain, not a tremble in his voice; it was as though it were not his back the machete was lashing, over and over again, shredding his skin. The brilliant eyes of the "Brother of the Faith" seemed to burn; his arms open to the sky seemed to draw down pardon for his executioners. He was at that instant an incredible, supernatural, marvellous man.' [22]

Loving God also encompasses obedience ... and the rewards are great.

Love's Rewards – Good from Evil

Kefa Sempangi has written a significant book that poignantly shares the real story behind the martyrdom of Christians in Uganda under Idi Amin. He concludes with these challenging words:

> 'The story of what God was doing in Uganda did not end with Idi Amin. What Pharaoh had meant for evil, God was

using for good. For every newspaper headline, for every story of atrocities and death, there was another story which went unreported and unnoticed. It was the story of those who, by faith, had "escaped the edge of the sword" and those who, by faith, "were slain with the sword." It was the story of how God's people, in the midst of great suffering, had come to understand the depths of love. And it was the story of how God, in His providence, had led His children into the wilderness, to prepare a table before them ...

Even with these thoughts I heard the voice of Dr K. as he said good-bye on our last evening together. "The whole world might turn against you," he had reminded me, "but Jesus Christ stands with you." ' [23]

The positive results of loving God wholeheartedly are many. One of the most important is the growing awareness that God will bring good from every terrible event and circumstance, personally and corporately. Actually this awareness and the principle of loving God above all else are in a symbiotic relationship – each promotes and supports the other.

A footnote for Romans 8:28 in the New International Version of the Bible caught my attention. It indicates that a valid alternate translation of the oft-quoted 'all things work together for good' passage is

'And we know that in all things God works together with those who love him to bring about what is good.'

How exciting!

I am reminded of interviews with Christian leaders in the former Soviet Union. They acknowledged that the pressures of the communists rather than destroying the church, actually purified and strengthened her. Christian youth were not allowed into communist-run universities but were also thus not contaminated by worldly philosophy.

The Tiananmen massacre in Beijing, China in mid-1989 was a brutal action against demonstrating students. Yet from the ashes of that disaster, thousands of students and intellectuals have come to Christ not only in Beijing but all over the country. Shortly after the tragedy, I met a group of Christian students who shared with me that you could not walk on their campus at any time without seeing a group of young Christians sitting on the grass having a Bible study together.

What an honour to work together with the God we love to bring about what is good. This is what Paul refers to later in Romans 12:21,

> *'Do not be overcome by evil, but overcome evil with good.'*

Love's Rewards – Father Care

Lucien Accad is the Director of the Bible Society in Lebanon. When the civil war began in his country, he recalls a trip to town when he took his five-year-old son along.

Shooting suddenly broke out. Panicky people were running for shelter. Lucien prayed for God's protection while trying to remain calm so his son would not panic.

After the situation calmed down, he questioned his son about his fears. The boy answered, 'Of course I was not afraid. Daddy, I was holding your hand.'

The war continued for many years. Lucien says, 'I have never forgotten those simple words of my little son. It has always reminded me that if I have my hand in the Father's hand I don't need to panic.'[24]

An important result of loving God is the depth of relationship it builds with our good and kind Heavenly Father. In Deuteronomy 1:31, Moses refers to the desert experience and says,

> *'There you saw how the Lord your God carried you, as a father carries his son, all the way you went until you reached this place.'*

Iranian Christian leader Mehdi Dibaj, spent nine years and twenty-seven days in prison. In early 1992, he wrote a letter to his younger son on his birthday. It reads in part:

'In a park a child will let go of his father's hand and joyfully and happily will go on to play and skip around him. He does not pay attention to the father calling, "Come my son, we must go." But if this was on a busy road, this same playful boy would not let go of his father and would stick ever so closely to him as if they were bound together...

Sometimes on a busy road, strong wind and heavy traffic make the crossing between streams of cars so frightening that the child's legs freeze and he begs his father, "Daddy, carry me! Daddy, carry me!"...

What a joy it is for a little child to sit on the broad and strong shoulders of his father! From that height he watches the passing of the time and the commotion of the world. What fun! Peaceful and happy like a satisfied baby resting in his arms!

On the earth, snakes, scorpions, dogs, and wolves get crushed underneath the powerful steps of the father, and the child "sticks closer to his father every time he gets frightened." Because "the rod and the staff of the father comfort him."' [25]

Margaret Fishback Powers wrote the following original lines at Canadian Thanksgiving time in 1964. She was then a young woman searching for direction at the crossroads in her life. They have since become known as *Footprints* and treasured by millions all over the world.

'One night I dreamed a dream.
I was walking along the beach with my Lord.
Across the dark sky flashed scenes from my life.
For each scene, I noticed two sets
of footprints in the sand,
one belonging to me
and one to my Lord.
When the last scene of my life shot before me
I looked back at the footprints in the sand.
There was only one set of footprints.

I realized that this was at the lowest
and saddest times of my life.
This always bothered me
and I questioned the Lord about my dilemma.
"Lord, You told me when I decided to follow You,
You would walk and talk with me all the way.
But I'm aware that during the most troublesome
times of my life there is only one set of footprints.
I just don't understand why, when I needed You most,
You leave me."
He whispered, "My precious child,
I love you and will never leave you
never, ever, during your trials and testings.
When you saw only one set of footprints
it was then that I carried you." ' [26]

Father, you have asked me to love you with all my
being – more than anyone or anything else. Forgive
me for my lack of wholeheartedness. Help me to
obey all your commands and truly love others –
even my enemies.

Thank you for your promise to make all things
work out in the end for good. And thank you for
your fatherly care – especially when you carried me
without my realizing it.

*The risk-free life
is a victory-free life.*

Jamie Buckingham

Secret Two –
Wholehearted commitment to God

Jesus who gave his all for you and me asks, no he demands, reckless abandonment and wholehearted commitment to the point of death from those who would be his disciples ... rewarding them with the overcomer's crown.

Chapter 2

Radical Risk-Takers

She waved away the acrid white exhaust smoke from the plethora of passing motorbikes and continued walking down the wide boulevard in Ho Chi Minh City, Vietnam. Mrs Ha's heart was still heavy. This visit with her husband in the prison seemed so short. Yet she smiled to herself as she relived that fleeting hour.

'How the authorities must grind their teeth over my husband,' she mused. They arrested him on December 10, 1983. Under his leadership, the Tran Cao Van church in Ho Chi Minh had grown dramatically. Although the church remained closed, most of the believers found their way into other fellowships and house meetings. And now in prison, he was having as much personal ministry as he had in earlier years of freedom.

She turned the corner and quickened her pace as she thought of her children waiting at home to hear news from their daddy. As she dabbed the perspiration beads on her face she saw them watching for her up on their balcony. How she thanked the Lord for that balcony. 'Isn't it just like the Lord to turn every bad situation into good?' she thought.

At the time of her husband's arrest, all their personal possessions were confiscated and she and the children were forced to leave the church parsonage and find their own accommodation. Then just two months ago, she had been forced by the city authorities to leave the apartment she and the children shared with another family from the church. Not having official residence papers was the charge.

Now the Lord had provided other Christian friends willing to share what little extra space they had in their small apartment – the balcony.

The children came bounding down the stairs both asking questions at once while waving a letter just arrived from close Christian friends who had emigrated to Ottawa, Canada.

After answering the children's many questions and giving a full report of her short visit with their father, she settled down to read the letter from Canada. The daylight hours were now long gone. But even though she was physically exhausted and emotionally drained, she felt prompted to get out her paper and pen and answer the letter. Part of her letter read:

'You know around here we are experiencing hardships. But thank the Lord He is supporting us and comforting us and caring for us in every way. When we experience misfortune, adversity, distress and hardship, only then do we see the real blessing of the Lord poured down on us in such a way that we cannot contain it. Hallelujah!

We have been obliged recently to leave our modest apartment and for over two months have been living on a balcony. The rain has been beating down and soaking us. Sometimes in the middle of the night we are forced to gather our blankets into our arms and run to seek refuge in a stairwell.

Do you know what I do then? I'm happy, I laugh, I praise the Lord because we can still take shelter in the stairwell. I think of how many people are experiencing much worse hardships than I am...

...I don't know what words to use in order to describe the love that the Lord has shown to our family. I only can bow my knee and my heart and offer to the Lord words of deepest thanks and praise. Although we've lost our house, we've lost our possessions, we have not lost the Lord and that is enough. **With the Lord I have everything.**'[1] (emphasis added)

In recent years, more North Americans can identify with Mrs Ha in suffering losses of one kind or another. In an era of job terminations, restructuring, forced early retirements, and poor health, we can relate to the problem. But do we relate to the solution?

My best friend, Dr Jim Cunningham, wrote an interesting paraphrase of Habakkuk in 1994 while patiently waiting for God to provide permanent employment:

'Though the job offers do not come
and there is no employment on the horizon.
Though the stock investments decline
and my RRSPs [2] produce no income.
Though there are no savings in the account
and minimum cash in my pocket.

Yet I will rejoice in the Lord.
I will be joyful in God my Saviour.
The Sovereign Lord is my strength.
He makes me walk on the edge with sure feet
and calms me to enjoy the view.' [3]

Jesus called his first twelve disciples with the brief but compelling imperative, **'Follow me!'** They left everything to follow him. Today his call is still the same but we know so much more. Those first disciples learned on-the-job. We have the benefit of all their recorded experiences as well as years of examples from church history.

Jesus' words still ring out loudly in the 1990s.

'If anyone would come after me, he must deny himself and take up his cross daily and follow me.' [4]

This pronouncement was made just moments after Peter had declared Jesus to be the Christ of God. Jesus warned his disciples to tell no one. He also predicted that he must suffer many things and be killed – but then raised to life again. In this context come these immortal words of our Lord to all who would be disciples. [5]

In our modern world, these words of commitment seem so

foreign that we must analyze them thoroughly to apply them to our comfortable and affluent existence. Someone has said, **'Today our bonfires of selfishness are fueled by the gasoline of affluence.'** Again there is nothing intrinsically wrong with affluence. But it has proven to often anesthetize us to the realities and demands of discipleship.

Tony Campolo was speaking to church youth leaders at Missionsfest in Vancouver, Canada. He quoted Jesus' words of self-denial and sacrifice in Luke 9:23 and then made this astute observation:

> **'You cannot communicate that in the comforts of the local church. That can only be accepted as a viable option when your young people are discussing it in the context of people who are suffering!'** [6]

Self-Denial

Alexander was alone on a ministry trip to assist the fast-growing church on the island of Cuba. At the beach resort where all the tourists stayed, a very attractive young lady tourist had her eye on him. One evening when she thought no one was watching she propositioned him to join her for the night in her room. He graciously declined.

But someone is always 'watching' in Cuba. And later an alcohol-ladened Cuban revolutionary challenged him.

'Heh, man. Why didn't you accept that beautiful girl's offer tonight. Wow, what a honey! What's wrong with you?'

Alexander replied, 'Yes, she is beautiful, but I'm married.'

'Sure, but you're a long way from home. Your wife will never know,' argued the revolutionary.

Pointing to the wedding band on his left hand, Alexander continued, 'But I made a commitment to my wife on the day we were married that I would deny myself the pleasure of any other woman. I wear this ring as a constant reminder and a sign of my commitment.'

The revolutionary was very touched. Though he was very committed to Fidel Castro and the revolution and was willing to die for the poor, he had not been faithful to his own wife. At that very moment he was in the middle of a messy divorce.

Because of Alexander's integrity, the revolutionary listened carefully through his alcoholic numbness as he heard for the first time that 'God sent his son to die the same way you are willing to die, except his death has the power to set you free in all areas of your life!'

Jesus said, 'Deny yourself!' He indicates that for his disciples there is a cost to be considered regarding our commitment to him.

King David set a pattern when he said,

> *'I will not sacrifice a burnt offering to the Lord that costs me nothing.'*[7]

The apostle Paul stated,

> *'I consider my life worth nothing to me, if only I may finish the race and complete the task the Lord Jesus has given me – the task of testifying to the gospel of God's grace.'*[8]

At Christmas in 1978, Jack Baker and I ran a Christmas contest on our FEBC 'Morning Coffee' radio program from Manila, Philippines. We asked our many shortwave listeners to write in 50 words or less 'What's the first thing that comes to mind at Christmas time?'

We were pleasantly surprised to receive an entry from the Peoples' Republic of Mongolia which read:

> 'When I think of Christmas the first thing that comes into my mind is its significance, especially in relation to the lives of myself and those about me. I think of what Christmas originally cost, of what its significance costs myself and others today.'[9]

Rather than discuss food, presents, or traditions, this listener could only think of what it originally **cost** God and Jesus. And what it **cost** himself and others in the Suffering Church at that time.

Dwayne Armstrong, a missionary leader working in the country of Egypt, told one of my co-workers, 'We have an urgent need for new workers. But I tell those interested, **if God calls you to Egypt, it's a collect call ... meaning you'll have to pay.'** (emphasis added)

The cost of serving Jesus is a personal one. It boils down to a powerful but unnatural attitude: Instead of insisting on my rights I am willing to forego them in favour of others.

This is a learned disciplined behaviour pattern because everything in our modern society mitigates against it. The world in which we live is diametrically opposed to any concept or practice of self-denial.

Others who think they understand it have a very warped perspective. For example, every Lenten season the newspapers contain stories of those who before Lent committed as much sin as possible in order to ask God's forgiveness and help to give up those sins for the next forty days. Self-denial may be popular among some during Lent, but Jesus called for a daily commitment to Himself in all areas of life!

Thus truly following Jesus today requires deliberate steps that may very well run counter-culture. Jesus concludes,

> '... *any of you who does not give up **everything he has** cannot be my disciple.'*[10] (emphasis added)

The popular devotional writer Oswald Chambers calls this the battle of 'abandonment'. He suggests that true abandonment to Jesus begins internally in the will rather than in the external world. 'I am determined to be absolutely and entirely for Him and for Him alone.'[11]

Giving yourself in true abandonment to him means refusing yourself the luxury of asking any questions. We have no ends of our own to serve. In fact, it never produces the consciousness of its own effort, because the whole life is taken up with the one to whom we abandon ourselves ... and then he works through us all the time.

Chambers says,

'There is only one thing you can consecrate to God, and
that is your right to yourself (Romans 12:1) ... Paul said he
knew how to be a "doormat" without resenting it, because
the mainspring of his life was devotion to Jesus
(2 Corinthians 12:15).' [12]

David Wang of Asian Outreach shares a powerful story about
a Chinese Christian he calls Martha. She was engaged to be
married but decided to postpone her marriage for two years to
answer the call of God to deliver Bibles where they were
urgently needed. David's own words tell the story:

'I recall meeting her once in the city of Xian. We had
arranged to meet at 9 p.m., but she did not turn up
until about 1 a.m. She was delayed because she had been
delivering Bibles in a nearby village. But the local
commune leaders discovered what she was doing. They
beat her up, robbed her, and threw her on a deserted road.
It was a miracle that she was able to make it to our
appointment.

I noticed something was wrong with Martha. She was
thin as a wire and her face was bloated. I asked, "What is
the matter with you? Did they beat you up like this?"

"Oh, no," she said, "I've had this problem for some time
now." Then she rolled up her pants to show me legs covered
with stings and mosquito bites. As she travelled in the
remote countryside of China, often she had to sleep in
deserted huts or even out in the fields. She was literally
eaten up by bugs and mosquitoes.

"Tomorrow we must go to a doctor," I urged her.

"No, no," she said, "I have to catch an early train tomorrow to go to Inner Mongolia. Where are the Bibles?"
Her only concern was to get the Bibles to Inner Mongolia!

In August 1983, Martha disappeared – as though she had
just vanished into thin air. That was during China's "Anti-
Crime Campaign" when many people were arrested and

executed throughout China. We became concerned for Martha.

Later we got a letter from her through her friends. It was not really a letter – just a little piece of paper. She had been arrested and charged for distributing "superstitious materials" in the People's Republic of China.

The little note read: "I don't know what the penalty will be, but please pray for me." She quoted Paul's words: "Pray for me that whenever I open my mouth, words may be given me so that I will fearlessly make known the mystery of the Gospel, for which I am an ambassador in chains" (Ephesians 6:19–20). A few weeks later, we received word that 24–year-old Martha had been executed. She paid the price.' [13]

Martha had put the Lord **first** over her marriage, **first** over her own safety, **first** over her own choices. She had denied herself.

Former co-workers Don and Marion Roberts, now of Couriers International, were making their first visit to the People's Republic of China. They met a wise old pastor who had spent more than twenty-one years in prison for his faith. When they discussed this subject and the lack of self-denial in much of the western world, he concluded, **'You must deny yourself now so that when you are persecuted and they make you deny yourself, you will be ready to handle it victoriously.'** (emphasis added)

Bear the Cross Daily

When our children were young, we would often sing before dinner the chorus, 'Come and dine the master calleth, come and dine...' One day our youngest, Melinda, an adopted Filipina asked, 'Daddy, why does Jesus say we have to come and die?' The family laughed at this question concluding that we really needed to work on our singing diction.

But as I study Jesus' teaching, I've come to realize that

Melinda was singing correctly all the time. Because Jesus also indicates that discipleship means there is a cross to bear.

All too often the cross becomes for us just an historical symbol. One day a North American minister was showing a foreign visitor his new church. He pointed with pride to the imported pews and other fancy trappings. Outside, a spotlight illuminated a huge cross on the steeple.

The pastor boasted, 'That cross alone cost us $10,000.'

The visitor looked at him quizzically and replied, 'Where I come from, Christians can get them for free!' [14]

A Canadian Christian aid worker was overwhelmed at the enormous need among the believers of southern Sudan. He recalls some children in a village wearing nothing but hand carved bone crosses fashioned in necklaces around their necks. He pointed to the cross on one emaciated child and questioned her with hand motions. She smiled broadly, took off the necklace and handed it to him.

His thoughtful analysis is this:

> 'That little act symbolizes the state of the suffering church in Sudan. With absolutely nothing in the way of material possessions, they still have the cross of Jesus Christ. They are prepared to share it's hope – even though it means death.' [15]

To Jesus the cross meant the willing denial of self for the sake of others. He taught that

> '...*unless a kernel of wheat falls to the ground and dies, it remains only a single seed. But if it dies, it produces many seeds.*' [16]

He then goes on to state the paradox which follows Luke 9:23. The person who seeks to save his life will lose it while the person who loses his life for Jesus will save it.

Dietrich Bonhoeffer, the German theologian who gave up his life taking a stand against Hitler wrote, 'When Christ calls a man, he bids him come and die.' [17] That's what it means to lose our life in order to save it. Jesus himself was our example, being willing to go to the cross on behalf of others – even a lost world.

A 'tentmaker' missionary in Morocco struggled with the issue of dying for Christ. He concluded with these words:

> 'Is faith in Christ worth dying for? I quickly saw that if it wasn't, I had no business presenting the Gospel to Muslims. You see, when a Muslim receives Christ, he faces certain persecution and possible death. How can I ask a Muslim to receive Christ as Lord if I have doubts in my own heart. **If Christ isn't worth dying for, He isn't worth living for.** On the other hand, if Christ is worth living and dying for, then we have a Gospel that is of infinite value to Muslims...
>
> Ahmed came to see me one day, honestly sharing his fears with me about following Christ. He asked, "What if I go to prison?" This kind of question had always intimidated me; I wasn't sure that I could ask someone to be willing to go to prison when I myself had never gone. Yet now I realized that it was Jesus who was calling him to take up his cross and follow, not me. This was between Ahmed and the Lord.'[18] (emphasis added)

Recently I learned about a thirty-two-year-old pastor who works in upper Egypt, an area of intense persecution for Christians. He runs a day care centre, a medical clinic and a literacy training program as well as caring for the families of those in prison. He has been beaten twice by Muslim fundamentalists and threatened daily with death. He knows they are trying to kill him – but he continues to daily bear his cross.

A leading pastor in Egypt shared about a parishioner who tearfully came for counselling. Young people she had trained at her work were recently promoted to be her supervisors. She was passed over solely because she was a Christian. The pastor concluded, 'That's the cross we must bear here in Egypt!'

The essence of these examples is that instead of exercising and asserting my will, I learn to cooperate with God's wishes and comply with his will.

I'll never forget visiting the house church of Pastor Lamb in Guangzhou, China with my wife Dianne in 1985.[19] That night we were introduced to his twenty-four-year-old assistant pastor. We soon learned that she had no 'danwei' or work-unit. This is how all people in China are identified and registered. Even some shopping requires a 'danwei'.

When asked, 'Isn't it risky for you to work full-time in a house church and not have a "work-unit"?' she simply replied, **'It's the way of the cross!'**

One of our Canadian couriers to Cuba asked a leading pastor who has received many greatly needed Spanish Bibles from us, 'We're placing you at risk, aren't we?'

He answered with his hand on his heart, 'Risk? What risk? I took a risk when I accepted the Lord Jesus Christ as my Saviour and became a minister. And if they want to shoot me, so much the better. I'll go into glory sooner.'

Rinaldo Hernandez is another Methodist pastor in Cuba. His father spent five years in prison for political subversion and wanted the family to escape to Miami. But Rinaldo decided that staying in Cuba was a cross he must bear:

> ' "I remember my father told me that I would pay a high price for that decision," he says. His price was to come later when his seminary education was disrupted by assignment to compulsory military service in a work camp. There conditions were primitive and most of the men were hardened criminals.
>
> He and seven other Christians met secretly at night in the sugar cane fields to pray, read the Bible and encourage one another. "I became a pastor in that work camp, not in seminary," he concludes.'[20]

Noted theology professor Dr Thomas Oden reported after visiting Cuba in early 1994,

> 'Although conditions have improved, being a Christian in Cuba is still a risky business. No one witnesses without peril. Hence, most Cuban Christians are willing to be

martyrs in the classic sense of that word. This charges every baptismal decision, even every church service, with radical seriousness. It helps the church to understand precisely what is its most important task and to examine all other options accordingly. Cuban believers are learning firsthand where their most compelling accountability lies: to their risen Lord.' [21]

A Cuban theology professor tells him,

'To be a Christian amid a struggling socialist system is a wonderful adventure. Here you can discover that the promises of God belong to you. You grasp this only when you rely under risky conditions upon those promises. They are best proved true for the faithful in difficult, challenging situations. Here the church must truly be the church or its identity will quickly be lost.' [22]

The late Jamie Buckingham made many memorable statements. One of them is:

'The risk-free life is a victory-free life. It means life-long surrender to the mediocre and that is the worst of all possible defeats.' [23]

A Chinese Christian brother from the north-west province of Xinjiang was released after serving twenty years in prison. He shared this poem written by his wife just before her death in prison:

'As a real disciple I have dedicated my life
Hoeing the fields energetically,
Begging for food shamelessly,
Wearing worn-out clothes as if they were formal dresses
Freezing to death at the windy station
Yet uttering not a word of complaint.
Only if the Gospel would be widely spread
Am I willing to be hung upside down on the cross
With no regret.'

Follow Me

The repetitive replays of the shocking videotape on all of Manila's television stations seemed endless. But what else could be shown of interest in light of the current event that shocked and numbed a whole nation – and most of the world. It was August 21, 1983. Opposition leader Benigno Aquino had returned to the Philippines only to immediately fall to an assassin's bullet on the tarmac of Manila International Airport.

During his exile in the United States, Aquino had shared with Chuck Colson about his new found faith in Jesus Christ. He was warned by Mrs Marcos not to risk returning to the Philippines. But he could not be threatened and he was prepared. He gave his life!

After the people's revolution of 1986, Mrs Aquino replaced the Marcos government as the elected president. A new five hundred peso bank note was issued with Benigno Aquino's picture and most remembered statement, 'THE FILIPINO IS WORTH DYING FOR'.

Jesus indicates in Luke 9:23 that discipleship also means there is a person to follow. And following Jesus fully means commitment and cost in every circumstance and situation.

One of Jesus' descriptions of his own lifestyle was the lack of a permanent bed. One day a man told Jesus that he would follow him wherever he would go. Jesus responded,

> *'Foxes have holes and birds of the air have nests, but the Son of Man has no place to lay his head.'* [24]

This verse did not really mean much to me until I met with Vasili and Galina Barats in Moscow in April, 1988. They had each spent years in the infamous gulags for their outspoken faith in Christ and their desire to emigrate to a land of religious freedom. But upon release, they were not given a residence permit for Moscow where they had earlier been living when arrested. A residence permit at that time was necessary for any housing, including hotel rooms. Other people were at risk when housing someone without such a permit.

The day before Easter Sunday, they secretly visited our group in our Moscow hotel and tearfully revealed that they had spent the previous night on the streets since they had nowhere to live. We all wept with them as they shared and prayed with us.

As we told them about the prayer campaign Christians had participated in for them during their imprisonment and more recent persecution, Galina broke down. Through her tears she uttered, 'Your prayers are the one thing that has sustained us through all these trials!'

Jesus' call also extends the concept of bearing the cross daily to willingness to follow His way step by step regardless of the circumstances – even to the death. Jesus Christ came to this world to die. Anyone who would truly be his disciple then should be prepared and ready for the same fate. But he promised that sacrificing life in his name would never be a waste.

Early Church father Tertullian was the first to be credited with the comment, **'The seed of the church is the blood of the martyrs.'** He was converted through the testimony of Christians singing on the way to their death. Later, he was credited with the statement, 'The more you mow us down, the more quickly we grow; the blood of Christians is fresh seed.' [25]

The book of Acts is punctuated with this concept. We are often reminded that the Greek word translated 'witness' in Acts 1:8 is the root word martyr. It is as if to say that martyrdom is therefore a witness by blood. Giving ones very life is considered the ultimate sacrifice.

Martyrdom though is not a totally unique concept to Christianity. Visiting Yad Vashem Museum in Jerusalem is a very moving experience. It is dedicated to the millions of Jews who lost their lives in the holocaust. One large poster sign caught my attention:

Sanctification of the Holy Name is fulfilled in three ways:
A. A Jew who sacrifices himself when forced to convert his faith.
B. A Jew who endangers himself in order to save one soul of Israel, more so to save many souls.

C.   A Jew who falls in battle while defending Jews.

Moses Maimonides had already maintained: A Jew that was killed even though not for the reason that he resisted conversion but only because he was Jewish – is called holy.

During the Tiananmen student demonstrations on early June 4th, 1989, eye-witness accounts tell of tanks and armoured personnel carriers moving toward the students' statue of liberty.

Two rings of 100 students each clasped arms around the statue yelling, 'We are not afraid to die; we are not afraid of giving our young blood for the future of our country; immortality will give us democracy.' [26]

Chai Ling was a key student leader during the occupation of Tiananmen Square. In a video-taped interview during the tensest days she said,

> 'What we are actually hoping for is blood-shed ... Only when the square is awash with blood will the people of China open their eyes.' [27]

A Muslim who dies in 'jihad' is considered a martyr and is the one category of Muslim assured of a definite place in paradise. A leading Islamic Jihad ideologue in Gaza says,

> 'Our young men are trained at an early age not to fear death ... They know it will come in 30 years or in five minutes. It makes no difference to them.' [28]

George Otis Jr in his monumental volume, *The Last Of The Giants*, states that Islamic fundamentalists claim that their spiritual revolution is fueled by the blood of the martyrs. He then questions whether Christianity's failure to thrive in the Muslim world is due to the notable absence of Christian martyrs.[29]

Christian martyrdom is not a phenomenon only from the early church period nor just the experience of those in the creative-access nations. Dr David Barrett, editor of the *World Christian Encyclopedia*, says there have been more than forty million Christian martyrs killed since AD 33. In early 1996, Dr Barrett published the annual average for Christian martyrdom worldwide at 159,000. [30]

What is most interesting is Barrett's estimate that a foreign missionary in the 1990s has a three percent likelihood of dying a martyr's death. He defines martyrs as 'believers in Christ who have lost their lives prematurely because of their faith, in situations of witness, as a result of human hostility.' [31] He predicts the number of Christian martyrs to rise to 500,000 annually by the end of the decade.

Dr Barrett goes on to say, 'For people in well-to-do countries to say, "How terrible this is," only goes to show how far they are from the apostolic way of life. **The normal church is the suffering church.'** [32] (emphasis added)

He concludes,

'Of course Christians should not seek martyrdom, neither can they control where it occurs or when. **But where it happens, the church is most truly following its Master.'** [33] (emphasis added)

Brother Andrew shares an experience from Eastern Europe when he was counselling Gerhard, a committed young Christian who was being drafted into the army where he had to take an atheistic oath and swear allegiance to the force dedicated to wiping out the church in his country. Andrew says:

'To Gerhard, that was a thing he would not do. He loved the Lord Jesus enough to be willing to say no, but there was no way to say no – or so it seemed. We discussed several options and in the end I said to him, "Gerhard, why don't you die as a martyr for Jesus!" And it was then that he jumped up and exclaimed, "Andrew, if only they would *let* me. I would *love* to die as a martyr for Jesus, but they won't let me. They'll convict me of some political or economic crime, but they won't let me die for Jesus." ' [34]

The noted missionary to India, Amy Carmichael, wrote in one

of her many poems, 'Can we have followed far, who have no wound or scar?'

Dick Eastman of *Every Home For Christ* shares the words of a young African man written shortly before he was martyred for his faith:

'I am part of the fellowship of the unashamed.
The die has been cast.
I have stepped over the line.
The decision has been made.
I am a disciple of Jesus Christ.

I won't look back, let up, slow down, back away or be
   still.
My past is redeemed, my present makes sense, my future
   is secure.

I'm finished and done with low living, sight walking,
smooth knees, colourless dreams, chained visions,
worldly talking, cheap living and warped goals.

My face is set, my gait is fast, my goal is Heaven,
my road is narrow, my way is rough, my companions are
   few,
my guide is reliable, my mission is clear.

I won't give up, shut up or let up until I have stayed up,
prayed up and paid up for the cause of Jesus Christ.

I must go till He comes, give till I drop,
preach till everyone knows, work till He stops me.
And when He comes for His own, He will have no trouble
recognizing me because my banner will have been clear!' [35]

Dead Already

Hossein Soodmand was the senior pastor of an Assemblies of God church in Mashad, Iran. He was the only ordained Iranian minister from Islamic background who chose to remain in Iran during the Islamic Revolution. After he had suffered repeated imprisonments for his faith, church authorities offered to help him leave the country to work in Greece or Turkey among the Iranians living there. He declined the offer saying, **'Don't break my heart. I count it a privilege to stay and undergo hardships and persecution for my Lord.'** On December 3, 1990, he was hanged by the authorities.[36] (emphasis added)

Even other Iranian Christians thought that the believers from his church would be frightened by this but just the opposite happened. The church in Mashad has grown five hundred per cent. One of Pastor Soodman's sons offered his life for training to replace his father.

During this time, Iranian Christian leader Mehdi Dibaj, spent over nine years in prison for his faith. In early 1992, he wrote a letter home on his son's birthday. Part of the letter reads:

> 'I don't want to hide it from you that I always envied those Christians who all through Church history were martyred for Christ Jesus our Lord. Because for a Christian it is a loss to leave this world by natural death. What a privilege to live for our Lord and to die for Him as well! And I am prepared for the name of Jesus Christ our Lord, not only to remain in prison but to give my life in His service as well.'[37]

His day was indeed to come. In late 1993, he was tried on charges of apostasy (from Islam) after being a Christian for over forty years. He made his own defense and simply used his written statement to share his commitment to Jesus Christ.

In early 1994, he was sentenced to execution. When his younger son (to whom he wrote the birthday letter) visited him he said,

> 'Please tell all who pray for me that I believe this is my hour of trial like Abraham ... I will not bow before the worldly-minded people and beg them for my release or forgiveness! I am quite ready for execution. This is my privilege that no one has the right to take away from me.'[38]

There was a great international outcry when the news of Mehdi Dibaj's scheduled execution was publicized. Suddenly on January 16, 1994, the Teheran government released Mehdi Dibaj from prison and denied it had sentenced him to death for converting from Islam to Christianity over forty years earlier.

It was a great day of rejoicing for the believers in Iran. When Mehdi Dibaj first met with them, their immediate response was to burst into song – 'In the name of Jesus, we have the victory!' Even *TIME* magazine reported the release under the title 'Answered Prayers'.[39]

But the international rejoicing was to last only three days. On January 19th, Assemblies of God Superintendent Haik Hovsepian-Mehr mysteriously disappeared en route to the airport. Chairman of the Council of Protestant ministers in Iran, Bishop Haik Hovsepian-Mehr had spoken out courage-ously against the persecution of Iranian Christians and the closure of the Iranian Bible Society as well as a number of churches across Iran. He had campaigned vigorously for the release of Rev. Mehdi Dibaj. He had acted as substitute father for Mehdi's four children during his imprisonment in addition to his own four children.

Only on January 30th did government officials contact his family to ask them to identify his dead body through a picture. They claimed they had found his body with chest stab wounds on January 19th and because of unknown identity they had buried it several days later. They did not follow the normal pro-cedure of a newspaper photo of unidentified victims.

Iranian Christians reported that the Bishop was a brave and humble man who was much loved and respected by the church community in Iran. They added that in his last few weeks of life, he would often speak about his possible martyrdom for which he was prepared. At his memorial service one of his taped sermons was played which spoke about giving your life for the sake of Jesus. One of his statements regarding the possibility of losing his life was made to Brother Andrew just weeks before he died, **'I will not die a silent death!'**

Two thousand people attended the funeral service. They heard Mehdi Dibaj say, 'I should have died and not Brother Haik!'

The day I received this shocking news of Brother Haik's death by fax, I was up early reading in Isaiah and came to the first verses of chapter 57:

> '*The righteous perish and no one ponders it in his heart;*
> *devout men are taken away, and no one understands that the*
>   *righteous are taken away to be spared from evil.*
> *Those who walk uprightly enter into peace; they find rest as*
>   *they lie in death.*'[40]

In early July 1994, Mehdi Dibaj's dead body was discovered in a forest. Christians in Teheran say there were rope marks around Mehdi Dibaj's neck that could indicate a hanging.

A few days later the dead body of Iranian pastor Rev. Tateos Michaelian who succeeded Bishop Haik as chairman of the Council of Protestant Churches in Iran was found. He had been shot in the head. His last sermon had stressed that Christians should be ready to be martyred for the name of Jesus Christ.[41]

Bishop Haik's brother, Rubik, told Open Doors' Prayer Conference attenders in October, 1994 that his brother's church in Iran had doubled in numbers since the death of Bishop Haik earlier that year.

Christians who consider themselves already dead have a tremendous liberation of spirit to do the work of the Lord without fear. Often they claim that it is only in this state of preparedness that a disciple can truly 'live for the Lord' with abandonment.

Dr J. Christy Wilson gave a paper at the historic Lausanne '74 conference. He shared about a Christian in another country who was returning where the punishment for conversion to Christ was death. He was asked whether or not he was afraid to go back. He replied, 'I have already died in Christ!'

Open Doors colleague, Hector Tamez, says this concept is amplified by Christians living in war zones of Latin America. The Christians caught in the civil war between the government and Shining Path guerrillas in Peru are a classic example for us. Here is how Hector expresses their commitment:

'They know that they are going to be killed. And they say, "In order to be a Christian here, you have to recognize that you are **dead already in Christ**. Once you recognize this, then any day that passes by in your life is a gain."

If you survive one year over there, then you have had one God-given year to testify not only with your words but with your deeds.'

The Chinese believers have a full hymn of six stanzas entitled **'To Be A Martyr For The Lord'**. The chorus repeats the title and ends with 'I am willing to die gloriously for the Lord.'[42]

In 1952, Ni Tuosheng – better known as Watchman Nee – was visiting friends in Hong Kong. Many urged him not to go back to China because of the hard atheism of the communist regime. But he had received a call from God to return and suffer together with his brethren. He was very clear about the path God had ordained for him. **'My end is not to be raptured, but to be martyred.'**[43] (emphasis added)

Exactly twenty years later he did indeed die for his Lord after much suffering in the infamous labour camps of rural China. His suffering was not without the fruit of impact for Jesus in many lives. And recent reports of his passing on indicate that other prisoners were so impacted by his testimony and love for Jesus, that some followed Christ even after his death.[44]

Victorious Overcomers

Dr Paul Negrut from Romania says,

'The heroes of Romania are those who died in their faith, those who faced the communist persecution and terrors with dignity, and died honoring Christ. It's because of those martyrs, their testimonies ... that we are experiencing the blessings of God.'[45]

Dr Negrut's spiritual mentor was Dr Joseph Tson. He experienced severe persecution and was ultimately expelled from the country. In freedom he often shared the significance of being willing to be a martyr:

'During an earlier interrogation at Ploiesti I had told another officer who threatened to kill me, "Sir, let me explain how I see this issue. Your supreme weapon is killing. My supreme weapon is dying.

"Here is how it works. You know that my sermons on tape have spread all over the country. If you kill me, those sermons will be sprinkled with my blood. Everyone will know I died for my preaching, and everyone who has a tape will pick it up and say, 'I'd better listen again to what this man preached, because he really meant it; he sealed it with his life.'

"So, sir, my sermons will speak ten times louder than before. I will actually rejoice in this supreme victory, if you kill me."

He sent me home.

Another officer who was interrogating a pastor friend of mine told him, "We know that Mr Tson would love to be a martyr, but we are not that foolish as to fulfil his wish."

I stopped to consider the meaning of that statement. I remembered how for many years, I had been afraid of dying. I had kept a low profile. Because I wanted badly to live, I had wasted my life in inactivity.

But now that I had placed my life on the altar and decided I was ready to die for the Gospel, they were telling me they would not kill me! I could go wherever I wanted in the country and preach whatever I wanted, knowing I was safe.

As long as I tried to save my life, I was losing it. Now that I was willing to lose it, I found it.

I was right that first day of interrogation: the Lord had taught me many lessons during those trying hours. Meanwhile, the secret police heard the Gospel and got to see the love of Christ in action. We both came out better as a result.

Jesus taught us long ago: with Him, the road down leads upward. With Him, the path of suffering ends in victory. The road to Calvary does not stop until resurrection.'[46]

Dr John Pitt was Open Doors' Director for Africa for many years. He often shares the testimony of Benjamin Dube, an evangelist who witnessed on Soweto streets of his faith in Jesus Christ. His message was that instead of hating one another, blacks must love whites and whites must love blacks. He was threatened many times. One day some black people approached him and commanded him not to preach about loving one another any more. 'We don't want to love our neighbour, we hate him!' they told evangelist Dube.

Benjamin carried on. One night he dreamed he was stabbed to death by his own people. He woke up his wife, Grace. 'I believe this dream is going to happen,' he said. 'We will have to decide whether to carry on and suffer or stop and, in doing so, disobey God.'

The following day they discussed the dream and also the constant threats with their children. 'Must I continue this message of forgiveness?' Benjamin asked his children. All four nodded although they were well aware of the consequences.

Benjamin Dube prayed together with his wife and children asking the Lord for strength to remain faithful. Not long afterwards, evangelist Dube had to preach at a meeting again. His children were with him. In the middle of Soweto his car was stopped by ten black men. They dragged the faithful preacher out of the car and stabbed a knife into his chest sixteen times. The children fled. Twelve-year-old Bonani hid behind a garbage can. He helplessly watched his father being repeatedly stabbed.

The murderers took Benjamin's Bible and dipped it in his blood and then disappeared into a dark street. Little Bonani ran to his father, but he was already dead. Bonani then rushed home to tell his mother the horrible news. Immediately he went to his bedroom and in his great need and sorrow called out to God. He opened the Bible lying near his bed. The first words he read were the words of Jesus on the cross, 'Father forgive them, for they know not what they do.' There in his bedroom he drew comfort from these words and composed a new music score to sing them.

Later the murderers were arrested. Seven of the ten were

sentenced to three months' imprisonment because they had only helped plan the murder, but were not directly involved. The others were given fifteen years.

After the funeral, Grace and her children got together and decided they would not stop sharing their message of love and forgiveness. Together with the children she continued to witness in word and song about the redemption of Christ.

About a year after the death of her husband, Grace and her children were holding an open-air meeting. The seven accomplices were on the loose again. After Grace and her children had sung a song, she gave her testimony. She ended with a call to repentance. 'Friends, begin a new life with Jesus. He takes away all hate and gives love in return. Come and talk to me if you want to follow Jesus.'

There was a movement in the crowd. Young and old came forward. Suddenly a man pushed through and stood with his head bowed before Grace Dube. 'I also want to start a new life with Jesus,' he said softly.

Grace looked at the young man and trembled. He was one of the seven accomplices who had planned the murder of her husband. He did not look at her. For a moment Grace did not know what to say. Then she put her arms around him and through her tears said, 'Now you are my brother!'

A deathly silence descended on the crowd. They had recognized the man too, and so had Grace's children. While everyone looked on, the children began to sing, 'What a mighty God we serve'.

John concludes that Benjamin Dube did not want to be only an on-looker and neither did his family. They would rather follow Jesus and die than be only spectators and live.

> *'They overcame him (the accuser of our brothers) by the blood of the Lamb and by the word of their testimony; they did not love their lives so much as to shrink from death.'*
>
> (Revelation 12:11)[47]

Lord, you have asked me to deny myself, take up the cross daily and follow you. Forgive me when I have been too self-centered to remember your demands ... or have followed but far off. Help me to live as though I had already died so that I will be willing to risk everything for your glory. Thank you for those whose lives have proven that you can also make me a victorious overcomer.

**If Christ be God
and died for me,
then no sacrifice can be too
great for me to make for him.**

C.T. Studd

Secret Three –
Wholehearted service for God

Because of Jesus' love and example for us, we prove our love for him as faithful bond servants — wherever we are placed ... and his reward is his personal presence with us always.

Chapter 3

Bloom Where Planted

The military truck swerved repeatedly trying to overpass the congestion of motorbikes in the streets of Ho Chi Minh City. Some of the small bikes held as many as five people – the whole family! Perched on a rough seat in the back of the truck, Pastor Ho Hieu Ha drew in his breath and wiped the perspiration from his face as the driver nearly toppled a 'family bike' in his careening path.

Pastor Ha thought of his own growing church membership. So many of them travelled like that to get to church or home worship centres. The memories made him smile.

It had been a year and a half now since his fast-growing church had been forcibly closed and he incarcerated. That was Christmastime in 1983. The smile became wistful as he contemplated the road ahead. Today was the beginning of his trial. Would his beloved wife and children be allowed to attend? He missed them so much.

The truck lurched to a stop in front of the courthouse. As his slender body stepped out of the truck, the brightness was almost blinding for a moment. He heard a murmur swell across what he now could see was a large crowd of people. As their faces became clear, he recognized many of his former church members. What loyal and faithful people they were!

Then he spotted his wife. A feeling of excitement filled him. He wished she could visit him regularly rather than just the few occasional sessions. But as his eyes made contact with hers, he noticed she was crying softly. How he longed just to hold and comfort her. He could tell she was worried about his obvious frailty and loss of weight.

Realizing that a great number of his former flock were there in the crowd and also needed encouragement, Pastor Ha called to her, 'Dear, please don't cry! There's no reason to cry! The Lord has given me as much ministry in the prison as I had before in my church. And I'm willing to stay and serve him.' [1]

In the preceding chapters we have encountered those who love Jesus so much they are willing to **die** for him. But there is also the other side of the coin where we are called to **live** for him. Dying to self is the liberating and energizing factor in living for Jesus. This accompanies a strong awareness of the power and majesty of God.

A letter from a ministry that has a burden and vision for North Korea has just arrived in the mail. It shares how a Korean national was on tour in the North. He contacted a group of secret Christians. Their greatest desire was water baptism and they asked him to help them.

They ensured no unwanted eyes by getting the guide drunk and then went to the river. The visiting brother had never baptized anyone before. In the unrehearsed questioning of the candidates he asked, 'Are you willing to die for Jesus Christ?' And they answered, 'Yes, and we are willing to live for Him!' [2]

In Kabul, Afghanistan, a young blind man listened to the gospel by radio. He had already memorized the whole Qur'an in Arabic, a feat comparable to our memorizing the entire New Testament in Greek. When he later publicly declared his faith in Jesus as the Messiah, his friends asked him if he realized that he could be killed for this since the Islamic Law of Apostasy for anyone leaving Islam is death.

He answered, 'I have counted the cost and am willing to die for the Messiah, since He has already died on the cross for me.' Zia then became the spiritual leader of the few Afghan Christians.

After studying at the Institute for the Blind, he became the first blind student to attend regular-sighted schools in Afghanistan. He completed high school, finishing two grades each year. He wanted to study Islamic Law so that he could defend

Christians who might be persecuted for their faith. He graduated from University of Kabul with his law degree. On the side he learned the German language and translated the New Testament into his own dialect.

Zia travelled to Saudi Arabia where he won a memory work contest on the Qu'ran. The Muslim judges were so amazed and chagrined that a non-Arabic speaker had taken first place, they awarded another prize for the best Arab in the contest.

Under the communist regime, Zia was arrested on false charges and put in the Puli Charkhi political prison outside of Kabul where thousands were executed. There was no heat in the jail to protect the prisoners from the cold winter weather. He had to sleep on the freezing mud floor in his overcoat. A prisoner next to him was trembling with cold since he did not even have a jacket. Zia knew John the Baptist had said,

> *'The man who has two coats should share with him who has none.'*　　　　　　　　　　　　　　　　(Luke 3:11)

He took off his only coat and gave it to the neighbour. From then on, the Lord miraculously kept him warm every night. He slept as if he had a comforter over him.

In prison the communists gave Zia shock treatments to try to brainwash him. The electric burns left scars on his head. But he did not give in. When he was offered the opportunity to study Russian in prison, he mastered this language also.

After release from prison, Zia learned Hebrew and the language of neighbouring Pakistan, Urdu. He continued translating the Bible, writing and preaching.

On March 23, 1988, Zia was kidnapped by a fanatical Muslim group, Hisbe Islami, and was accused of being a CIA agent because he knew English, a KGB agent because he knew Russian and an apostate from Islam because he was a Christian. He was beaten for hours with rods ... A blind person cannot see the club coming and thus gets the full force, even like the torture the Lord Jesus experienced when he was blindfolded and then struck (Luke 22:64).

The recent word is that Zia Nodrat was cruelly martyred. He

will not only be remembered for his martyrdom, but also because he lived his whole life to serve the one who was his Lord.[3]

Bond Slaves

Romanian pastor Paul Negrut shares a prayer written by a Christian prisoner just before he died by execution under the communists of Romania. His paraphrased translation reads like this:

> 'Lord, I look forward to the great day I see you and your family in heaven.
> I look forward to seeing the great evangelists standing before you.
> I look forward to the day I see all the missionaries coming home rejoicing with their sheaves.
> I look forward to hearing all the great singers of the world praising you.
> I look forward to seeing the great preachers of the ages standing before you.
> But Lord, I have one special request.
> When that day comes, allow me to be there in the clothing of a prisoner.
> I want to praise you throughout eternity in my prisoners clothes to always remind me that I was a prisoner for you.'[4]

Christians in the Suffering Church visit brothers and sisters in prison regularly. One reason is for the encouragement they bring. Another is that they can bring much needed gifts of food. There are numerous reports how these visiting Christians would stand outside the prison or camp after their short visit and sing at the top of their lungs. I was encouraged to read one such song translated from Chinese into English as follows:

> 'I'm a little bird in a cage, away from the trees, flowers and fields.

To be in bonds for you, Lord, how glad I am to sing and
   pour out my heart to you all day.
You like to hold my wings that like to fly.
Listen to the songs that I have to sing;
Your great love constrains me, **I'll be your love slave
   who will never run away**.
Who will understand the bitterness of prison life?
But the love of the Lord can make it sweet;
Oh, Lord, I love the road You have prepared for me.
May the whole creation praise your wonderful deeds.'

(emphasis added)

The Christian prisoner for whom this was sung 'stood on the balcony and wept, touched beyond measure.'[5]

In the New Testament, the apostolic writers continually referred to themselves as slaves of Jesus Christ or 'bond servants'.

In Bible times, slaves had no rights. But a slave or 'bond servant' had the right to leave his master after he had worked off his indebtedness. If out of love for his master he chose of his own freewill to stay and become a lifetime member of that home, he went through a strange but agonizing ceremony. His master would literally nail his ear lobe to the doorpost of his house with a hammer and small spike. The spike or awl was immediately removed but the ear hole and scar remained as a symbol of his commitment. It was a sign like a wedding ring – only much more demanding – saying, 'I love my master and have given myself for him so I can give myself to him.' From then on he was a man marked for life as belonging to that house.[6]

In the *Hermitage* in St. Petersburg is a painting depicting 'The Baptism of Jesus'. Brother Andrew writes about his experience there 30 years ago:

'The museum guide points to the beautiful painting and says, "In the background there are groups of people standing who were made slaves by this man." This communist had seen it correctly: Jesus doesn't make slaves for a system, no members for a church, no supporters for a religion or followers of a philosophy.

He said: "Follow me", and those followers became **slaves** of the Person of Jesus Christ. Then they could, and dared, to put up their lives for him. They had given *everything* and therefore couldn't lose any more. Now they could go wherever he sent them.' [7] (emphasis added)

As I write this chapter, I'm staying at a Christian youth hostel in Lausanne, Switzerland. The husband of the couple who serve as house parents has a favourite sweatshirt he wears often which states in large letters, **'JESUS IS MY BOSS'**. And in the O of the word 'BOSS', small letters say 'I'm styled by Jesus Christ'.

The Suffering Church has a significant understanding of being bond servants and styled by their master, Jesus. They realize that to be a disciple is to be a devoted bondservant motivated by love for the Lord Jesus.

Serve where Placed

Vietnamese Pastor Ha is an amazing example of willingness to serve Jesus wherever He places you – even a cockroach-infested prison with rotten food. Here is his own description of that experience:

'If God had called me to prison ministry in 1975, I would have refused. But He spent those years preparing my heart, so when the time came, I accepted. I saw all this as the amazing plan of God.

During my six years and twenty-three days of living in the iron cages, the Lord called ninety-six people to believe in Him. They were members of the former government, officials from the new communist government, refugees, Chinese, Cambodian – even a few of our captors.

My prison wasn't like one in the United States with television sets everywhere. We slept on the cold floor, facing mosquitoes, leeches, and cockroaches. Prisoners were always hungry, fighting disease constantly and battling each other.

One time I was isolated in a very dark room. For sixteen months I didn't see anything. The food was rotten. But praise God, I wasn't sick once during that period.

God put me in prison to share Jesus Christ with the outcasts and the hopeless to express his love. His glory became known in that prison. The guards tried many ways to keep us from communicating with one another, but the witness went on.

Over the years, the prisoners had dug holes in the thick walls from one cell to another. Their purpose was to pass cigarettes, but I used them to speak about the Lord. When I was in isolation, I found that the people below me could hear through the toilet hole. They memorized verses of the Bible, learned songs and came to Christ – all through that hole.'[8] (emphasis added)

Later Pastor Cuong Nguyen also spent over six years in prison in Vietnam before being deported to the United States. Over one year of that time was spent in solitary confinement. The rest alternated between periods of boredom and intense interrogation day and night. He says that the lesson he learned from his imprisonment was, 'Wherever God puts you, that is your mission field.' During his prison term he led fifty-six people to faith in Jesus Christ. Many of them are active today as Sunday school teachers.[9]

I find the commitment of these pastors extremely liberating. But they were not the first who impacted my life regarding prison ministry. While living and working in Singapore in the mid-eighties, I read the amazing testimony of a Nepali Christian leader who refused to be intimidated by imprisonment for leading others to Christ in that Hindu kingdom. His name was Pastor Nicanor Tamang. I'll never forget my amazement reading his prayer request to believers in the West. He said, 'Don't pray that I will be released from prison!'

My western orientation could think of no other way to pray for him. Yet he could see – though a family man – that God had placed him strategically. Later I had the joy of meeting him and his family personally in Canada and learning more of the details of God's anointing on this special brother in that prison. Actually church leaders in Nepal now worry that without the threat of imprisonment the church may lose its courageous passion for evangelism.

Tirtha Thapa, general secretary for the National Churches Fellowship in Nepal, tells about one visit he made to Christians in prison:

> 'As I entered, the light was dim and it was difficult to see. I could make out shapes in one corner of the cell, huddled together against the cold, on the bare concrete floor. As my eyes adjusted, the battered faces of the men came into focus. They were bound together with wire that pierced their hands and wound around their limbs, causing intense pain. They were miserable looking creatures. I had met them before on a previous visit, but in their present condition I didn't recognize them. But they recognized me. "Jaya mashi!" they shouted. "Victory of the Messiah! ... Don't worry, we're fine, singing the song of the Lord. Tell our brothers and sisters we're happy here in police custody."' [10]

Power in Chains

China's church patriarch, Wang Ming-dao, was questioned after his more than twenty-three years in prison for the Lord. One interviewer asked, 'If you had not been in prison, wouldn't you have done more work for the Lord?' He answered, 'No, the work that I did by staying in prison is greater than I could have done by not being in prison.' [11]

Somehow there is power in chains! Even the Apostle Paul expressed that so clearly in Philippians 1:12–14. He indicates that what most other Christians thought would be so terrible – his own imprisonment – God turned into good. Rather than hindering the spread of the gospel, it actually aided its advance. And as a result everyone including the palace guard learned that

Paul was in prison because of his love for Christ. And more importantly he said,

> '*most of the brothers in the Lord have been encouraged to speak the word of God more courageously and fearlessly.*'[12]

The prisons outside North America have an infamous reputation for physical cruelty, mental torture and inhumane conditions. Yet from all over the world come reports of Christians who saw their imprisonment as an opportunity to serve their Lord. The documentation is so overwhelming an entire volume could be dedicated to just this point.

In Addis Ababa, Ethiopia, fourteen Christians continued their witness while in prison by reading Scripture aloud. By the time they were released, they had read through the entire New Testament and forty-four inmates professed faith in Jesus Christ.[13]

Prison inmate Pedro Pablo Castillo preached and counselled political prisoners in Nicaragua. Eventually almost half of the four thousand prisoners in Jorge Navarro jail near Managua became Christians. On the eve of their release, seven hundred political prisoners prayed, sang and read Scripture to celebrate their pardon. Castillo returned to the jail prior to his former cellmates' release to urge them to 'let Christ shine' in their lives whether 'in jail or outside.'[14]

Armando Valladares in his moving book, *Against All Hope*, shares about a Christian prisoner in Cuba who deeply impacted his own life and faith:

> 'His hat fell off his head and the wind ruffled his white hair. Very few men knew his real name, but they knew that he had an inexhaustible store of faith. He managed somehow to transmit that faith to his companions, even in the hardest, most desperate circumstances.
>
> "Faith, brother," he constantly repeated, and he left a wake of optimism, hope, and peace. All of us called Gerardo the Brother of the Faith. He was a Protestant minister and had dedicated his life to spreading the word of God. **He was his own most moving sermon.**'[15] (emphasis added)

Mrs Chen from China had a similar experience during her first imprisonment:

'As she sat quietly singing a hymn, the Lord gave her a message: "This is to be your ministry."

"But," she objected, "I am all alone. Whom can I preach to?" She continued to pray that her ministry would be fulfilled. Suddenly an idea came to her. She stood up and called for the guard.

"Sir, can I do some hard labor for you?"

The guard looked at her with contempt, mingled with surprise. No one had ever made that kind of request before.

"Look!" she exclaimed, "this prison is so dirty, there is human waste everywhere. Let me go into the cells and clean up this filthy place. All you have to do is give me some water and a brush."

Not to her surprise, she soon found herself on her hands and knees cleaning and preaching. She was looking into the faces of people no longer recognizable as human beings. Through continuous torture, they had lost all hope of ever seeing another human being who did not come to beat them.

"Oh, when they realized that they could have eternal life, they would get so excited. They would fall down on the dirty floor and repent of their sins, and do you know that very soon all the prisoners believed in Jesus Christ."' [16]

Pastor Matta Bush served over seven years of a thirty year prison sentence in the country of Sudan. Just recently a co-worker was able to visit him after his miraculous release. It came after his sentence was reduced to ten years and he had been transferred to a different prison.

He exhibited serenity and joy as he commented:

'God ... wanted me in prison for a special purpose. Many people are saved in prison ... In El Obeid prisoners were really saved and they began their new journey with God. Even the guards were also saved and that is why they transferred me here to El Khobar prison.' [17]

It turns out Pastor Matta Bush had thirty to forty people in a discipleship class in the former prison. He concludes, 'Because God loves me and I love Him, He gave me freedom to speak and preach in prison. Since there was nobody else, He used me to do His work!'

He shares that in the new prison, in the past two years over two hundred came to Christ through a Bible study class that prison authorities allowed him to lead. The prison authorities even gave permission for the construction of a chapel on the prison compound.

Shortly before his final release from prison, the prison authorities told Matta Bush that he did not really belong in prison. He was a good man, a man of God. And so they offered him the opportunity to go out of prison during the day. Of course, he had to return for the night. He accepted this at first and went out to meet some of his Christian friends in Khartoum. Then he realized this was not the will of God. How could he witness to his fellow prisoners who did not have this freedom to go out? And so he returned to the authorities and told them he would no longer make use of the opportunity to go out. He said it was clear to him that it was not yet God's time.

Later, they offered Matta another special privilege ... to sleep in a room which was air conditioned. He turned this down as he realized that this would mean he could no longer witness to his prison mates during the night – the most fruitful period to share. Matta himself called these two opportunities his two biggest temptations.[18]

Even young children from Christian families show an amazing understanding of this principle. The children of one family in China were asked, 'Aren't you sad that your father has been in prison for such a long time?'

They replied, 'How else would those in prison have been able to hear the Gospel of Jesus?'[19]

One of our African co-workers named Solomon was assigned to find out if there were many Christians in prison or labour camps in Mozambique. During his research, he was arrested himself:

'In prison, all my possessions, including my Bible were taken from me. Then I was subjected to a cross-examination for six hours, after which I was thrown into a cell, exhausted. I had to sleep on a concrete floor. I did not even get a blanket . . .

Knowing that my heavenly father would never forsake me, I directed all my attention to my fellow-prisoners. Although I still had to sleep on the floor and was harassed by malaria, bugs and a gnawing hunger, I tried to talk about my faith as much as possible.

After a Christian had managed to smuggle a small Bible into my cell – probably one I had brought into the country myself – I had the opportunity to preach to my companions. I prayed for the sick and the Lord heard my prayers and healed them. That was of great support to them and during my stay in prison, I led fifteen people to the Lord.

Unexpectedly, I found out that there were more Christians in prison. Now it became clear to me why I had to be arrested. In the first place to bring the message of salvation to the lost ones in prison and secondly to strengthen my fellow Christians.' [20]

Another Vietnamese pastor who was recently released from a long prison experience shares how the prisoners are made to wear a uniform with the letters CT printed on the front. The Christian prisoners wear this uniform with pride. In Vietnamese the letters stand for 'Cai Tao' which means 're-educated'. But to the Christians the letters CT also stand for 'Con Troi' which means 'Son of God'. [21]

Ignatius of Loyola is best remembered for his prayer:

**'Teach us, good Lord, to serve you as you deserve;
to give and not to count the cost;
to fight and not to heed the wounds;
to toil and not to seek for rest;
to labour and not to ask for any reward
save that of knowing that we do your will.'**

I Am Always with You

'[Ivan] shuddered, remembering the nightmare progression of cells: the cubicle with icy water pouring from the ceiling, and after that, the refrigerated cell, and then the agony of the pressure suit. "Jesus Christ is going into battle." As the words turned over and over in his mind an overwhelming sense of Presence jarred him alert. Joy spread gently through him, warming, burning, bringing him to his knees in the water. "For me you are to do battle. But be of good cheer. I am with you. I have overcome the world" ... Tears soaked Ivan's face. He bowed as low as he could in the cramped space, and wept and worshipped.'[22]

These words written by Myrna Grant in her moving biography of Russian martyr Ivan Moiseyev graphicly portray a theme to similar experiences I have noticed in my research.

Francisco, an elderly Cuban theology professor says,

'The Jeremiah narrative is especially instructive to us in Cuba. The Lord addresses Jeremiah in jail: *"Call to me and I will answer you and will tell you great and hidden things which you have not known"* [Jeremiah 33:3]. The Bible does not say, "Call to me and I will make you free." The Hebrew says I will show you not just magnificent things, but difficult and mysterious and inaccessible things, things otherwise out of reach to your slender imagination. Jeremiah has helped Cubans choose to be survivors amid this situation.'[23]

How clearly I remember sitting around a small kitchen table in Moscow with my travelling companion Carl Lawrence in early 1988. We were face to face with one of the Soviet Union's most renowned dissidents who had just been released from over eight years of harsh prison experience. I was amazed at the softness of voice and attitude as Aleksandr Ogorodnikov shared with us in detail his recent experiences.

He revealed no bitterness nor revenge. In his slow, halting English he said,

'I spent 176 days and nights in punishment cells and isolation. The floor was covered with water. The sewage system was deliberately blocked off, therefore excrement would flow out into the cell. The only way to avoid it was to sit on a short concrete post. In winter, the temperature in the cell never rose above freezing. You sat on the concrete floor without any underclothing. It was terrible.' [24]

Carl Lawrence has written so capably the continuation:

'Then he couldn't talk any longer. His eyes filled with tears, and he put his head down as he said, "Some days were so long." He paused, pulled a bit on his beard and continued, "Sometimes the hours were so long..." More tears. "Sometimes the minutes were so long..." A long pause. "Sometimes the seconds were so long." It was then that he looked up to the heavens and said, "But it was alright ... it was alright."' [25]

It was alright because Aleksandr sensed time and again the very presence of Jesus Christ in that cell. As a Russian Orthodox Christian who does not use evangelical clichés, he nevertheless attributed this blessing to those involved in intercessory prayer on his behalf. After his release he wrote:

'But it was in those terrible moments in icy cells that I **physically felt the warmth of your prayers and compassion**, a force linking us by a stream of spiritual energy generated by mutual experience of faith and the mysterious bonds of fraternal unity.
It was like the warm touch of a brotherly hand, which had moved aside the strands of barbed wire and penetrated through gloomy walls. The strength of your love and compassion turned my despair into indestructible hope, my

cries into prayers, and the edge of madness into enlighten-ment.'[26] (emphasis added)

Others are much more direct in their assessment of that 'warm presence'. A Christian in Pakistan named Gul Masih was recently in prison for his faith. He was condemned to death on a charge of blasphemy against the prophet Mohammed. In prison he wrote a long letter to those who prayed for him. Part of it reads as follows:

'My dear friends, my Lord has come to me twice in my prison cell. One day I was sitting in my prison and thinking about this injustice in a sad and hopeless mood. Suddenly my cell was filled with light and my body trembled. **I saw my Lord**. Four days after this, my Jesus came again and overshadowed me by raising His hands and blessing me. From that day on, I have been happy and in peace. **My Lord is with me in jail. He does not leave me alone**...'[27]

Oswaldo Magdangal is a Filipino Christian who worked in Riyadh, Saudi Arabia and pastored a secret house church. There has not been an official church of any kind in Saudi Arabia for over fourteen hundred years.

In late 1992, Oswaldo was arrested with a co-worker after a raid on their meeting place by the 'muttawa', the Saudi religious police. For three-and-a-half hours he was physically and mentally tortured.

They slapped, boxed and kicked him on the face. Then using a long stick, they lashed his back and the palms of his hands. Then the soles of his feet. He could not stand without wincing and he describes his bruised body as looking like an eggplant.

Upon returning to his cell, Wally prayed for five hours thank-ing God for allowing him to participate in the sufferings of Jesus. Here are his own words:

'Suddenly there was light. The cell was filled with the Lord's Shekinah glory. His presence was there. He knelt and started to touch my face. He told me, "My son, I have seen all of it, that's why I'm here. I am assuring you that I will never leave you or forsake you." ' [28]

He awoke two hours later feeling like a new man. He was amazed when he saw his body had been restored to perfect wholeness. No bruises, no cuts, no bleeding or blood stains. He adds, 'God had completely restored me.'

Miraculously, he and his companion were spared execution on Christmas Day. At the last moment they were deported home to the Philippines. Today he travels the world sharing about God's love and mercy.

Fourth Man in the Furnace

Biblically, the imagery often used is the fourth man in Nebuchadnezzar's fiery furnace. Chinese Christian Ding Xianggao says she too encountered a fourth man in her furnace during imprisonment:

'"It is not a fearful thing to go to prison because the Lord is with us," Ding says. "We know that the fiery furnace is a fearful place, but we need not fear. The 'fourth man' always appears and gives us indescribable joy." ' [29]

Shortly after his release from prison in Iran in early 1994, Mehdi Dibaj shared with an Open Doors co-worker:

'Those days were the best days of my life – walking so close with the Lord in the time of troubles ... It is wonderful to be in the fire knowing that you are not alone. You are with the Son of God like Daniel's friends ... When the Lord is with us, the prison is Heaven. It is Paradise. So I'm very grateful to the Lord for those opportunities. Indeed the best times of my life was in jail because I was with the Lord – really close! ... Wherever the Lord is with us, that place is Paradise. Praise the Lord!' [30]

The Chuguyevka Pentecostal Christian community in Siberia spent much effort in encouraging those of their brothers who were in prison. On one occasion they played hymns and poems through loud speakers for all the prisoners on the inside. The Russian language poem translates as follows:

'Wherever a storm of unbelief blows,
a hurricane batters the sanctuary,
then listen, church, your Saviour calls,
his voice like lightning through the sky.

Oh wretched person on whom this deluge descends,
you are being tested by these storms and struggles.
But love, gained in exile,
will conquer with its superior strength.

Joy of my Spirit,
you have grasped the calling of the Bride.
That's why we travel this road together,
this road that began in Golgotha.

And when you are torn from your loved ones,
because of the sentence they gave you,
I'm still with you in the Black Raven,
and behind barbed wire fences too.

My name wasn't mentioned at roll call,
neither yesterday or today,
Yet in your suffering I'm as close to you,
as the breaking waves are to the beach.

I too work in the stone quarry, like you,
I too work in the sawmill, like you.
I rejoice: your spirit has not been crushed,
you shore up your words with your deeds.

When you bed down on your bunk,
I kneel at your head and behold your face.
The whole night My love surrounds you,
together we greet the morning.

Beloved, endure yet a little while,
do not weep because of sorrow and pain.
I am coming, I stand at the gate already,
and triumphantly I welcome you into My Kingdom.' [31]

The reality of Jesus' constant presence is witnessed by more than just Christian prisoners. Yet it does seem to be in trying times that the believer senses the reality of this divine promise.

The Olson family are Lutheran 'missionaries' in Mazar-i-Sharif, Afghanistan – perhaps the most unlikely and illogical place for a Christian family to locate. But they are there to serve their Lord!

After Christmas 1993, they were confined to the basement of their dwelling for two weeks due to the fighting in their city. In response to the fighting and confinement, their eleven-year-old daughter, Lois, penned this insight:

'On January number two
Endless loads of bullets flew.
The news is on the BBC.
They still fought on January three.
Billows of smoke from someone's home?
How agonizing it must become!
Here we sit, we are quite safe,
When a man is mourned by his wife.
Many, many have sadly cried
Over someone that has died.
But we are safe: God protects us
And He has said He'll never leave us.' [32]

Lord, you have asked me to be your bond servant and serve you wherever you place me. Forgive me for always wanting to be in my own idea of a 'safe place'. Help me to see the opportunities you have given me even in trying and difficult circumstances. And thank you that you have promised to be with me wherever we serve together.

**Joy is the
gigantic secret of the Christian.**

G.K. Chesterton

Secret Four –
Enjoy the trip

Being in absolute surrender to God and filled with his Spirit to overflowing, we pilgrims can truly be persons of contagious joy... regardless of the struggles of this earthly pilgrimage or the pressures of refining persecution ... and are rewarded by God's protection.

Chapter 4

Enjoying the Trip

He was exhausted. And he longed to return to his hotel room in China's Zhejiang Province. But the Spirit prompted this Open Doors colleague to make one more visit. He arrived very late at Brother Wang's, a Chinese co-worker who was just recently released from prison. Wang insisted on telling him about the trials and challenges he had faced after being caught with Bibles and Christian literature while passing through a routine road check.

'I tried to remain calm,' said Wang, 'as the officer pointed at my seven full bags. I was arrested when he examined the contents and taken to jail for three months of interrogation.

'The prison cell was 150 square feet which I shared with 17 other prisoners. The only windows and ventilation holes were small slits in the walls.

'I became sick from the poor conditions. Yet the daily interrogations continued with the threats becoming more and more stern. I was repeatedly told I would never see my wife again.

'I was almost losing hope,' continued Wang, 'Then one day, while in prayer, I saw a vision of God. **He told me this world is not my home and Jesus had already prepared a place for me in heaven. Complete peace then flooded my whole being. I sang and gave thanks to God.**

'Suddenly I heard someone call my name. It was a prison guard. He told me, 'Pick up your bag – you're free!' I walked out of the detention center a free man with no charges filed against me.'

Our Open Doors colleague was now wide-eyed, his tiredness forgotten. He asked Wang what he expected to do now. Wang amazed him with plans for another Bible delivery trip – only days after his release.[1] (emphasis added)

This report comes to me while visiting the beautiful country of France. I am travelling with my colleague, Gilles Besson, who teaches me French as we drive many long hours per day from area to area on an Open Doors speaking tour.

When the weather is clear and there are beautiful Alps to view, no words – other than exclamations of awe – are uttered. On those other days when it is raining or foggy and all there is to view from the motorways is the treeline hour after hour, we have to work harder to 'enjoy the trip'.

The classic contemporary question is 'Are we having fun yet?'

One of the most notable characteristics of the Filipino people, among whom I lived for twelve years, is their uncanny ability to find ways to make any drudgery experience into fun. They really taught me how to enjoy any trip.

Our adopted Filipina daughter, Melinda, loves to repeat the Smurf family's experiences. While travelling in the car the children frequently repeat the well-known query, 'How much longer Papa Smurf?' And he patiently replies, 'Not much longer, children!'

Time-bound human beings have always expressed concerns about their perception of God's timing also. It has most often been expressed in the phrase 'How long, Oh Lord?'

Writers of the Psalms repeat over and over this concern for how long they must wait for God to reveal Himself;[2] wait for answered prayer;[3] or wait for God's justice to be seen in the world – especially against the unjust.[4]

Many of the Old Testament prophets cried out to God **'How long, Oh Lord?'** Most notable are Jeremiah and Habakkuk who both lived through very trying personal and national circumstances.

But the most plaintive cry is the final time that the question is put to God. In Revelation 6:10, the martyrs of the faith call out in a loud voice asking how long they must wait for God to avenge their deaths. The answer is most revealing.

'Then each of them was given a white robe and they were told to wait a little longer, until the number of their fellow servants and brothers who were to be killed as they had been was completed.'[5]

Only God knows the end from the beginning. Meantime his creatures are asked to patiently wait for His appointed time.[6]

Waiting patiently is not a cultural characteristic of Westerners. On my first visit to Cuba, one brother said, 'You North Americans are so funny. You all have watches but you have no time. We have no watches but we have lots of time!'

The clock in our family room is inscribed on the face with the words of the Psalmist,

> *'Teach us to number our days that we might apply our hearts unto wisdom.'*[7]

Joni Earickson Tada speaking at Missionsfest in Vancouver, Canada asked 'What does it mean to number your days?' She went on to say:

> 'I think it means to move through your days with measured steps. You're not in a marathon! The Lord tells us to keep in step with the Spirit. Move through the day in measured moments...
>
> You have a chance with twenty-four hours to live a day as you've never lived it before – totally unique and separate and distinct from all the rest. Packed with potentials and possibilities. God gives you that twenty-four hours to invest in a thousand-years-worth of eternal opportunity.'[8]

The day after writing the preceding part of this chapter, I am looking out the window for the first time at the awesome stillness of Israel's Dead Sea. But my mind and emotions are churning negatively because the airline I took here from Paris lost my suitcase and my briefcase (I handcarried my laptop so at least I can still write!).

Life is a lot like these extremes for everyone, especially the

Suffering Church. I have rarely met Christians with as true a sense of enjoying the trip – despite their many trials – as those in the restricted countries of our world.

Pilgrims

A Christian mother in Russia said to her son,

> 'The difficulties I have experienced in life have all left behind some really joyful memories, because God always helps us in our suffering. The pilgrim who eventually reaches his goal is no longer burdened by memories of the hard times past.'[9]

The most frequently used verbal imagery of life's journey is also biblical – that of being a pilgrim. Believers in Russia told me on my early trips that it was easy for them to hold earthly things very lightly when they viewed themselves as pilgrims on this earth. They said, 'We're pilgrims and we should always be reflecting our citizenship that is in heaven.'

The Scriptures have repeated references to this. The New International Version uses the word 'alien' where the Authorized Version used 'pilgrim'.

The best definition of a pilgrim I have found is, **'an intense narrowing of all our interests on earth, and an immense broadening of all our interests in God.'**[10]

Most of us from North America have no idea of the meaning of being a pilgrim. The closest we come to understanding the term is at Thanksgiving when we remember those who made sacrificial pilgrimages to this continent from Europe centuries ago.

Having just visited Israel, I was amazed at our Jewish guide when we were ascending the hills to Jerusalem for the first time. She said, 'Coming to Jerusalem – even for those of us who live here – you always feel like a pilgrim!' Indeed, I began to understand the concept more fully in that historic – and to many – holy city.

F.W. Boreham writes about Abraham Lincoln's life and death

in his classic, *A Temple of Topaz*. On that fateful night at Ford's Theatre in Washington, the President

> 'leaned forward, talking, under his breath, to Mrs Lincoln. Now that the war was over, he said, he would take her for a tour of the East. They would visit Palestine – would see Gethsemane and Calvary – would walk together the streets of Jeru...!
>
> But before the word was finished a pistol shot – "the maddest pistol-shot in the history of the ages" – rang through the theatre. And he ... turned his pilgrim feet towards the holiest heights of all.' [11]

Dr Stephen Olford in his great preaching on holiness says,

> 'We're pilgrims and we should be reflecting our citizenship that is in heaven ... We're to be holy as pilgrims ... As pilgrims we must present ourselves to our Heavenly Father who keeps us pure.' [12]

Dr Ken Taylor in his Living Bible translates Hebrews 11:13–16 as follows:

> *'These men of faith I mentioned died without ever receiving all that God has promised them; but they saw it all awaiting them on ahead and were glad, for they agreed that this earth was not their real home but that they were just strangers visiting down here. And quite obviously when they talked like that, they were looking forward to their real home in heaven. If they had wanted to, they could have gone back to the good things of this world. But they didn't want to. They were living for heaven. And now God is not ashamed to be called their God, for he has made a heavenly city for them.'*

Malcolm Muggeridge states this concept so powerfully:

> 'As Christians we know that here we have no continuing city, that crowns roll in the dust and every earthly kingdom

must sometimes flounder, whereas we acknowledge a king men did not crown and cannot dethrone, as we are citizens of a city of God they did not build and cannot destroy. Thus the apostle Paul wrote to the Christians in Rome, living in a society as depraved and dissolute as ours. Their games, like our television, specialized in spectacles of violence and eroticism. Paul exhorted them to be steadfast, unmovable, always abounding in God's work, to concern themselves with the things that are unseen, for the things which are seen are temporal but the things that are not seen are eternal. It was in the breakdown of Rome that Christendom was born. **Now in the breakdown of Christendom there are the same requirements and the same possibilities to eschew the fantasy of a disintegrating world and seek the reality of what is not seen and eternal, the reality of Christ.'** [13] (emphasis added)

When my three younger brothers and I were teenagers, we sang acapella quartet together. The lyrics of a favourite gospel song of the era were 'I can't feel at home in this world any more'. The first verse is indelibly in my memory:

'This world is not my home I'm just a passin' through
My treasures are laid up somewhere beyond the blue
I know He'll take me home though I am weak and poor
And I can't feel at home in this world any more.'

Pilgrims who pass through territory en route to their permanent home do not drive in their stakes too deeply. They know they are leaving in the morning.

The Christian should never feel a permanence here on earth. Jesus indicated that we are to be in the world but not of it. [14] Even he the Creator was not at home in his creation. In John 1:10 we read,

'He was in the world, and the world was made by him, and the world knew him not.'

But unfortunately instead of pilgrims with a clear vision of our final destiny, we are being labelled 'earth-bound tourists searching for the latest spiritual high.' [15]

One Chinese Christian stated it like this, 'We pilgrims carry small back packs!' [16] And this is because of a solid conviction that Jesus is soon returning with His reward for those who are found faithful.

Eighty-two-year-old Pastor Allen Yuan in China, like many others, has not retired because he could not find any reference to retirement in the Bible. He says,

> **'Jesus is coming back soon! We must work hard while it is still day, because the night is coming when no one can work.'**

Richard Halverson eloquently sums it up this way,

> '. . . the people of God are pilgrims and aliens in a world ruled by the rapacious god of deceit, intrigue, and murder – Satan . . . **Comfortable conformity to the world in which we live today may be the most subtle form of Christ denial.**' [17] (emphasis added)

Overflow of the Spirit

A significant dimension the Suffering Church brings to this concept is the awareness of the need to be filled with the Spirit of God. They often describe it as Scripture does – an 'overflow' experience.

Chinese pastor Allen Yuan often enthuses about the love of the brothers and sisters in China's Church. He says, 'This is an overflow of the Holy Spirit's presence in your life. A natural product of the Spirit-life.'

I still remember one of my childhood Sunday School teachers asking the class if a glass of water she had filled was really full. We were convinced it was. She added drops of water to our growing amazement. She vividly taught us that the only evidence of the glass being truly full was when the first drop overflowed down the outside of the glass.

Suffering Church members that I have interviewed are convinced that the greatest evidence of the filling of God's Spirit in the believer's life is the 'overflow' of the power and fruit of the Spirit from his or her life.

These are the modern day saints who also really understand what it means to '...*fill up in my flesh what is still lacking in regard to Christ's afflictions*...'[18] They understand the real significance of 'filling up' and the awareness that there is always something yet to be done.

Even a rough trip can be enjoyable when joy overflows from the Spirit's presence. Singing is one evidence of an overflowing life. It takes a lot of the stress out of the trip. And it smooths over many of the rough places in the road – especially when we sing praises to the God who created us and the world in which we live. The one who cares for us each mile of the journey.

Hebrew pilgrims sang Psalm 121 as they walked to Jerusalem each year to celebrate the feasts. This psalm helped pass the time on the way. It also reminded them of the many ways God took care of them. In the psalm are four word pictures that help God's people see him as the one who keeps them secure on their journey through life.

In Deuteronomy 32, Moses taught a new generation of Israelis a long song which he wrote for them. Its purpose was to show them that God deserved their love. The song called them back to him when they came to the end of their own strength.

The overflow of singing praises amid great difficulties has tremendous spiritual power for helping to enjoy the trip. Paul and Silas set the biblical pattern in the prison in Philippi.[19]

Pastor Jack Hayford enjoys sharing the story as told by his favourite black preacher. Paul and Silas' prison cell singing was heard all the way to the throne room of God. He began to tap his toe to the music. And since heaven is his throne and the earth is his footstool, that toe tapping created an earthquake!

Ivan Antonov spent twenty-four years in Russian prison camps for preaching the Gospel. He later shared how he survived:

'I would sing hymns. I was really glad that I knew so many. I had memorized about one hundred seventy hymns, and in order not to forget them, I reviewed several every day. So over a time, I sang through all of them. I want to emphasize to my young friends that you should worship God with songs and poems and memorize them. They will come in handy ... I sang hymns every morning and at night before going to bed ... In those quiet [morning] hours, I would go outside in the fresh air and sing hymns of praise to God and pray. Then I went in for breakfast with everyone else.'[20]

China's notable pastor Wang Ming-dao shared upon his release from prison that he frequently sang praises to God to buoy his spirits. The songs that meant the most to him were 'All The Way My Saviour Leads Me' and 'Safe In The Arms Of Jesus'.

His contemporary, Pastor Allen Yuan, shared with me two songs which he repeatedly sang aloud throughout his many years in prison. One was 'The Old Rugged Cross' and the other 'Psalm Twenty-Seven' from the Chinese Psalter. It is an emotional highlight to hear him sing these songs even today.

Pastor Ung Sophal sat in a filthy Cambodian prison badly beaten. His hands and feet were chained for five months. 'Only my mouth was unchained,' he said. '... So I sang to God in prison all the time. Another prisoner heard me singing through a small hole in the wall, so I taught him the song – a bit at a time. He passed it on and soon eight of us were singing.'[21]

Archbishop Dominic Tang spent twenty-two years in prison in China for his faith. He reports:

'Besides my prayer and meditation, every day I sang some hymns in a soft voice: "Jesus I live for you; Jesus I die for you; Jesus I belong to you. Whether alive or dead I am for Jesus!" This hymn was taught to me by a Protestant prisoner who lived in my cell.'[22]

Bill Harding IV shares personal experiences from Ethiopia where believers have suffered severely:

'In 1990 "perestroika" which had already spread through-out eastern Europe, filtered over to Ethiopia, and the Ethiopian government restored freedom of worship. The underground Church surfaced!

Church leaders suggested we use a meadow in front of our home for the first church conference in eight years, and we agreed. We expected about a thousand people from the underground churches to show up for the gathering, but more than 10,000 men, women and children – some having walked for two or three days – came from all over southern Ethiopia to join in the giving of thanks for their new free-dom. Never will we forget the singing and the preaching of those four days – often in a deluge of rain.

One night Grace and I were awakened by a loud clap of thunder and rain pounding on our tin roof. But then we began to hear another sound – **the sound of their voices praising God in song!** With tears in our eyes, Grace and I looked at each other. There were not words to speak the emotion we were feeling as we thought of these dear committed soldiers of Christ, many having undergone persecution and suffering, praising God in their joy at meet-ing publicly for him. Praising God for the rain. Praising God in spite of their discomfort!' [23] (emphasis added)

Occasionally elements in our own society reflect similar senti-ments. Stuart Hamblen wrote a popular gospel song which expresses that life is a short pilgrimage. Heartaches along the way are stepping stones along an ever upward winding trail. The chorus repeats the theme:

'Until then my heart will go on singing
Until then with joy I'll carry on
Until the day my eyes behold that city
Until the day God calls me home.'

Suffering – the Way to Joy

Alexander was on his first research trip to Cuba for Open

Doors. He asked a Cuban pastor what his needs were. He expected the response to itemize the many material needs that the churches in Cuba obviously lacked.

'The first thing we need is your prayers,' he replied, 'to know the Body of Christ is with us.' Then he went on to list their tremendous need for Bibles, teaching aids, Sunday School materials and writing supplies. Then he concluded with the statement that they could use anything and everything.

'If you send us just a bar of soap, we'll be grateful,' he confessed. 'We'll praise God for it!'

Alexander says, 'I felt a big lump in my throat as I thought of all the Bibles, literature and freedoms I enjoyed. Yet even with all my blessings, my testimony was not as strong. So I struggled to articulate my feelings. "Pastor," I said, "I can only begin to sense and imagine the difficulties you have encountered." '

The pastor's eyes became misty and he softly responded, 'Oh yes brother, we have been through a most difficult twenty-five years. Yet we don't fear persecution. As a matter of fact, we welcome it because it purifies us!' [24]

This is also the testimony of believers who suffered severely in China. 'The Lord knows. Suffering, testing, persecution, running from danger, and arrest can purify us. We should always be ready to receive God's discipline.' [25]

Freddie Sun spent years in prison in China because of his Christian faith. Prison was literally a trial of fire for him. He worked in a factory making tee-joints from pig iron. Every day he loaded and unloaded the furnace which fired up to 2700 degrees Fahrenheit.

In the midst of this hell on earth, God spoke to him. 'I have put you in this high-temperature furnace. Don't worry – you won't melt but your impurities will be removed so you can become a useful tee-joint!' [26]

Pastor Lamb of the largest known house church in Guangzhou, China says,

'A Christian without suffering is like a child without schooling.' [27]

This is another of the many paradoxes or apparent contradictions of the Kingdom of God. I well remember the story about the young boy helping a butterfly that was struggling to escape from its cocoon. But it couldn't fly and soon died. He later learned that the struggle to free itself is a necessary part of the development of the butterfly's wings.

'The best example of how to handle persecution comes from the first-century Christians who had their property confiscated and then were thrown into jail for their faith ... They knew the meaning of the words *aliens* and *strangers*.' [28]

The writer of Hebrews says about them:

'You sympathized with those in prison and joyfully accepted the confiscation of your property, because you knew that you yourselves had better and lasting possessions.' [29]

Noted Canadian Bible expositor Keith Price says,

'It is our capacity for suffering, not our capacity for joy, which is the more precise measure of how closely we are following Jesus. **Yet, oddly enough, the way to joy is through suffering ... We do not pursue happiness directly. It is always a bi-product of holiness. And holiness seems to attract suffering.**' [30] (emphasis added)

Another contemporary theologian, Cornelius Plantinga Jr, concludes,

'We do not want suffering; we want success. We identify not with those who are low and hurt but with those who are high and healthy. We don't like lepers and losers very well; we prefer climbers and comers. For Christians, the temptation to be conformed to this world is desperately sweet and strong. Yet, says the apostle Paul, we are children of God *if* we suffer with Christ ... **God does not give his hardest assignments to his weakest children.**' [31] (emphasis added)

Many people are positively challenged by the testimonies of

North American Christians who suffer with a positive attitude. Charlie Weedemeir is totally paralyzed except for his face muscles. He cannot talk. But through the lip reading of his faithful wife at his side he says, 'Difficulties come to everyone, but we always have a choice. **Pain and suffering are inevitable but misery is optional!**' (emphasis added)

A Chinese brother suffering in prison for his faith sent a message home to encourage his family. He wrote in poetic form on a fragile piece of toilet paper:

'Suffering often brings joy;
Daniel was tried by the den of lions and the furnace.
Since days of old there has been order in suffering and
   joy:
After you have emptied the cup of suffering,
Then comes the cup of blessing.
How can a son not receive chastening from his father?
A gardener's pruning has no ill intent;
Only to ensure that the tree bears good fruit.
Without fire, how can impurities be separated from gold?
Without striking the iron, how can it become a utensil?
Without chiselling, how can jade become a piece of art?
Without pressing, how can grapes become wine?'

Suffering – the Way to Witness

An elderly Christian engineer in a Nanjing factory was made to sweep the floors and clean the spittoons and toilets during China's infamous cultural revolution. There was hardly an accusation meeting where this pitiful whitehaired old man was not a target.

But he willingly suffered persecution, not giving way in the slightest. Other people were amazed because they all knew that if he would only denounce his faith once, he would be restored to favour and even promoted. Yet he would not comply.

A young engineer in the same factory, the daughter of a high-ranking cadre, observed him and then went home and told her younger brother, 'Surely there must be a God in this universe.' A few years later her brother believed in the Lord.

This happened all over China. Grains of wheat fell into the ground and died ... but later brought forth an abundant harvest.[32]

One Chinese Christian shared about the revival sweeping through his province which came in response to intense persecution of believers. He concluded:

> 'This rich life does not exist in a comfortable environment. Where there is no cross there is no crown. If the spices are not refined to become oil the fragrance of the perfume cannot flow forth, and if grapes are not crushed in the vat they cannot become wine. Dear brethren, these saints who have gone down into the furnace, far from being harmed, have had their faces glorified and their spirits filled with power, with great authority to preach the Word, and a far more abundant life...'[33]

The godly old man of the Romanian church, Trian Dors, once said to an Open Doors co-worker, 'I don't ask you to pray that we will avoid persecutions. On the contrary, it is our lot. Pray that we can endure and take advantage of the opportunities for witness that only intense persecution brings.'

Open Doors colleague Hector Tamez, loves to share the testimony of Sister Pasqualita who spoke at the 'Mexico, I Love You' Congress in 1993. She had suffered severe ostracism in her small town in the very southern part of Mexico because she had become an evangelical. Other Christians had already been forcibly driven from the town.

One night a group of her persecutors surrounded her grass-roofed home setting it on fire. As she opened the door, someone fired a gun at her. Hector says:

> 'When she was sharing her testimony she was crying. She said, "I thank the Lord that only twenty-one ammunition bits touched me." She had been shot all over her body and even in the neck. She was still able to run and fell into a

hole where her persecutors couldn't see her in the dark. She was losing blood quickly but some other townsfolk who appreciated her testimony somehow took her out through the mob to another nearby town's clinic. She survived but three other family members in the house were murdered.

She complained to the Lord saying, "Lord, why now that I've given you my life and my family am I suffering this way?" The Lord reminded her of a song that she used to sing very often, "**I have decided to follow Jesus, no turning back.**'

She continued, "Then I understood that when I decided to follow Jesus, it was in the midst of any situation, any persecution. My life now belonged to Him. I gained strength in that song. I am preaching again and I am encouraging the rest of the believers that when we decide to follow Jesus there is no turning back." When we heard this testimony, I can tell you we were crying.' [34] (emphasis added)

Cuban Christians have a favourite joyful hymn that's titled from Spanish 'In the Midst of Trials, The Church Moves Forward'.

Just recently I had the joy of meeting Pastor Dinh Thien Tu, the senior minister of the largest house church movement in Vietnam. During his two-year imprisonment during the early nineties, his house church movement grew from 3,000 people to 12,000 regular members, with some 13,000 others awaiting training and baptism.

'Persecution is not a major issue for most Vietnamese pastors,' says Tu. 'It comes with the territory. It's part of our normal church life.' [35]

Eastern European Christians who have lived under tremendous persecution have concluded, **'We Christians are like nails. The harder you hit us, the deeper we go in the Lord!'**

Chinese Christians express it this way:

'Christians are like the bamboo. It makes no difference how fierce the storm is or how cold the winter. It makes no difference how often we are cut down. We always sprout again and come back. Not as individuals but as a Body. And every time that Body rises, it rises stronger, more capable of giving life than ever before.'[36]

Pastor Mehdi Dibaj in Iran said, **'We Christians are like flowers. The more you crush us, the stronger the fragrance.'** And again, **'We Christians are like rubber balls. The harder you throw us down on the floor, the higher we rebound!'**

Submission – the Way to Freedom

The unrelenting interrogation persisted for ten days. As Timothy entered the offices of the Chinese Public Security Bureau for another intense eight-hour session, he sensed an overwhelming presence of the power of darkness. Fear gripped his heart. His hands and feet grew cold.

He was asked repeatedly to reveal the names of colleagues participating in Bible distribution in Shanghai. Fearing he might dishonour the Lord or harm a brother or sister in Christ he cried out, 'Lord, I yield to you. I lay down myself and my all on the altar, prepared to be chopped into pieces and burned.' Only then was there peace in Timothy's heart, his fear released by the power of God's Spirit.[37]

We only gain our freedom when we submit to his Lordship.

True discipleship is the surrender of one's whole life to the master in absolute submission to his sovereignty. The puritans referred to this principle as 'abandonment'. A speaker I heard recently said, 'We don't need more commitment but we do need more surrender.'

Perhaps this is the most profound spiritual principle of all. It encompasses all the other aspects of spirituality. For example, the best description of a person filled with the Holy Spirit of God that I've come across is **'a strong family likeness to Jesus Christ and freedom from everything that is unlike Him.'**[38]

Russian Pastor Herman Hartfeld shares, 'An old servant of the Lord was once in prison with me. I asked him, "What do you think prayer is?" Surprised that I should ask such a question, he replied, **"Prayer means that you hand your whole**

being over to God and don't want anything other than His will".' (emphasis added)

Pastor Mikhail Khorev prayed this way on his way to imprisonment in the former Soviet Union:

'O Lord my God, the point of my life is to glorify you in this world. Therefore take control of me and through me do whatever you deem to be the best for your church and for your glorious name.

O Lord, if my imprisonment will bring you more glory than a life spent in freedom then why should I choose freedom? ... And if you, O Lord, have ordained that I bring you more glory in court in the USSR, then why send me to the pulpits of the West? And even if my death should bring you more glory than my life in freedom, then why should I choose freedom?' [39]

Ironically, Pastor Khorev had more freedom in Christ than many of us who live in the so-called free world will ever know.

I remember my pastor one Sunday sharing about riding the mules down the paths of the Grand Canyon. The pathway is steep and treacherous. The mules are confident in their knowledge of the path. Thus the only safe option is to take your hands off the reins.

'Make me a captive Lord,
And then I shall be free;
Force me to render up my sword,
And I shall conqueror be.

I sink in life's alarms
When by myself I stand;
Imprison me within thine arms,
And strong shall be my hand.' [40]

Providential Protection

Mehdi Dibaj from Iran was at one time a missionary to neighbouring Afghanistan. There he soon became friends with blind believer Zia Noodrat. They were both very effective in sharing their overflowing faith.

One night as they said grace over their food, their prayers were extended due to a common concern. While they prayed, the cat ate the meat from their waiting dinner plates. When Mehdi opened his eyes, the cat was writhing in agony on the floor. The meat had been poisoned.[41]

Both men were later martyred for their faith but only when it was God's time. Until then they were miraculously protected by their heavenly father.

In Sudan, a young Christian girl recently converted from Islam was under much pressure from her brothers and sisters. They were in fact planning to kill her and bury her in the backyard so no one would know about it.

The day they planned to carry out their scheme she fell on her knees and prayed to God for protection. But to her siblings she responded, 'Kill me if you like, I know I will go to heaven!'

For an unknown reason they did not carry out the scheme but wrote a letter about her to their father. His recommendation was not to kill her but marry her off to a Muslim man who would keep her in the house.

They made the appropriate arrangements but on the wedding day the man did not show up and the marriage plans were cancelled. Later they found out the man was caught stealing and thrown into prison.

The next man died suddenly the night before the planned wedding. The brothers and sisters became terrified that any more attempts might backfire on them so they have left her alone and allowed her to go to church. She credits God with keeping her alive.[42]

Pastor Dennis Rutyigirwa of the Baptist Church in Kigali, Rwanda, tells how he and his family miraculously escaped being slaughtered in the 1994 holocaust:

'Just before the massacres, the party in power started arming the youth in Rwanda (the *interahamwe*) and giving them military training.

About five hours after the death of the president, we were warned on the radio to stay indoors; we learned that there were roadblocks all over. It seemed as if everything was well planned in advance.

The *interahamwe* went killing from house to house – you could hear people crying. Whoever ran from their houses were also killed.

We stayed home and prayed. My wife wanted to flee, but I told her to stay with me. **"If our time to die has come, we will not escape. If it is not our time, the Lord will protect us.'**

More than 20 militiamen burst into our house. One of them held a machete against my chest. They took my wife aside and held a knife to her neck.

I pushed my attacker away and shielded my wife with my body. "In the name of Jesus Christ, I won't allow you to kill my wife," I yelled.

He asked how many children we had and I said two. Again, I shouted, "In the name of Jesus Christ, we are not enemies!"

Trembling, he said to his troops. "Let us not kill these people. We can return later."

They told us to stay inside then went off to loot other houses. I sent my wife and children to the bedroom and sat in the living room reading the Word of God.

In Acts, I read the promise, "I have spared you that you can witness to others what I have done for you, and therefore you should not fear." Reading this filled me with courage.

Later the militiamen returned, pursuing someone who had escaped and run through our yard. They accused me of trying to hide people, and dragged me through the house to search it. They found no one except my family.

We heard shots all through the night, then the next day we were rescued by soldiers.'[43] (emphasis added)

Pastor Rutyigirwa concludes with his message for the church around the world:

'Be awake so that you will not be taken unawares as we were. If Jesus comes and it takes us by surprise, as the battle here did to us, it will be a sad day for the whole church.' [44] (emphasis added)

Lord, you have asked me to use my time wisely, be surrendered to your will and hold lightly the things of this world – to be a pilgrim en route to the holy city. Forgive me for my worldly focus and concentration on this life and its cares. Fill me with your Holy Spirit and give me an overflowing life – especially your joy. Thank you for your promise to take care of all my needs – even my very life – until the day you call me to be with you forever.

*We will have all eternity
to celebrate the victories
but only a few
short hours before sunset
in which to win them.*

Amy Carmichael

Secret Five –
Spiritual strength for the battle

The whole armour of God is needed to
stand against the devil's schemes . . .
but the Word of God internalized, and
Spirit-led prayer will enable the believer
to strike offensively . . . and with
perseverance remain victorious even under
the most difficult attacks.

Chapter 5

Strength for the Battles

Ukrainian pastor, Stepan Germaniuk was emotionally distressed as he sat in the prison cell. His mind kept replaying the crying of his three-year-old child (the youngest of five) earlier that day. The boy was upset that his father was so roughly taken away to the police station.

He relived the scene of the prosecutor showing him the three thick files of his case and demanding, 'Just renounce all your religious activities and I'll throw these files into the fire and you can go free!'

But Stepan smiled as he recalled the response that God's Spirit put into his mouth. 'I can't make such a promise. I can't stop serving the Lord.'

And now as evening was coming on, seven of the nine men sharing his prison cell were taken out. He was left alone in the cell with a man who was obviously insane. Stepan shares this horror in his own words:

'I got really concerned. As soon as all the others were out of the cell, the other man tore off his clothes and started coming toward me. He was in a complete rage, and I could see that he planned to attack me in a filthy way. I started to pray and said to him in a loud voice, "In the name of Jesus Christ I order you to get away from me!"

He was a tall strong man, but he immediately backed away. After a little while he started to close in on me again, and once more I ordered him in Jesus' name to get away.

This went on for hours. I was tense and alert and prayed as hard as I could. I could not stop watching for even a minute because he would attack me.

Later I learned that the prison administrators were observing the whole scene through a peephole in the door. They had evidently made a deal with this man beforehand that he would do this to me. But after I had repeatedly called on the name of Jesus Christ to order him away, and he helplessly withdrew to the corner each time, the authorities came in and took him away, naked as he was.' [1]

Throughout his many years of prison camp and later years of exile, Pastor Germaniuk was repeatedly tested and tempted to compromise. His triumphant conclusion is that 'since the Lord is with us, we know that victory is sure.'

In my experiences with the Suffering Church, spiritual warfare is very much understood and accepted as a daily part of the believer's life. But in studying my notes and journals, I came to realize they rarely discuss the topic outside the context of the positive spiritual disciplines that bring victory – what the Apostle Paul in Ephesians chapter six calls the armour of God.

The armour is to enable a believer to stand his ground in perseverance – to be strong, protected and equipped. Much of the armour is thus for defensive strategy. But two items are also vital for offensive activity: the Word of God, and Spirit-led prayer. [2]

God's Word Internalized

When China's best-known pastor, Wang Ming-dao, was finally released from prison he stated, 'In these past 20 years, I have not had a copy of the Bible. Happily between the ages of 21–24, I spent my time at home doing the housework and studying the Scriptures. I memorized many passages. These passages in my heart came out one by one and strengthened me. Had it not been for those words of God, then not I alone, but many others would have been defeated too.'

Pastor Lamb in southern China was in prison for many years

at that same time. 'I understood then why I had memorized so much of God's Word while in Bible school,' he says. 'I kept my sanity only by repeating Bible verses over and over.'[3]

In John Bunyon's classic, *Pilgrim's Progress*, Christian's pilgrimage is repeatedly threatened by satanic forces, human giants and worldly influences. But Christian is able to use the Word of God and the encouragement of fellow believers to be victorious.

Following the Psalmist's advice and hiding God's Word in our heart is the foremost weapon we have in this spiritual battle. And Christians in restricted situations seem to be more aware of this principle. Christians who spend many years in prison without a copy of the Bible leave an indelible impression of the importance of memorizing God's Word.

In the former Soviet Union, Pastor Ivan Antonov spent a total of twenty-four years in bonds for preaching the Gospel. He was released from Siberian exile in November 1988. In looking back he says:

'Most important of all, you should study and memorize the Word of God. When I was in prison and camp, I had no Bible, but I was able to review what I had stored in my heart. I went over two chapters from the Old Testament and two chapters from the New Testament every day.

This experience reminded me of Joseph in Egypt. During the time of abundance, he was laying aside stores of grain. When the famine came, he distributed grain from these stores, and the people were saved from starvation...

These Scriptures were food for my soul ... God always woke me up early in the morning ... This gave me time to pray and to meditate in peace.'[4]

Another Russian brother, Veniamin Markevich, reported upon his release from prison camp,

'...my main comfort and encouragement [while in prison] came from the Bible chapters I had memorized. These verses gave food to my soul and helped in the struggle against the demonic powers ... Those were just such "evil days" when special strength was needed in order "having done all, to stand" ... '[5]

When Laos was dominated by a communist government in 1975, the leading pastor Rev. Sali was put into a prison camp for three years of 're-education'. He referred to it later as his university experience. During that time he led five men to Christ in the camp. He had no Bible so he discipled these new believers on scriptures he had memorized and internalized. Later those men became leaders in the Church.

Over and over the Scriptures direct us to meditate on God's Word. That activity takes time and discipline. But its rewards are many – even for those outside prison walls.

A Singaporean colleague shared his debriefing with me after his first trip to China. He was most impressed with a large group of house church believers who memorized one chapter of the Bible every week. This process began due to a lack of Bibles but continued after they realized the blessing it brought to their lives.

This is also a method of qualifying believers to receive Bibles under short supply. In most restricted countries, there still is a significant lack of Scriptures. When Open Doors couriers provide some, the pastor is often in a quandary as to whom of the many spiritually needy he will share these precious books.

One house church group in Vietnam decided to give them to the believers who were most determined to use them. The criterion used was memory work. So Bibles were shared only with those who recited flawlessly Psalm 119 – all 176 verses!

No wonder we in Open Doors are so committed to provide God's Word to those for whom it is not available. And it is the power of God unto salvation!

During the years when I worked with the Far East Broadcasting Company in the 1970s, we received a letter from a listener in Vietnam after the communist takeover. It read, 'Brother, praise the Lord for the power of His Word. The more violently the storm rages, the more diligently people will search God's Word.'

Chinese Christians in southern China who in 1980 requested one million Bibles from Open Doors (known as Project Pearl) were so desirous of God's Word, they created a prayer song which they reportedly sang daily:

'Lord, send a Bible for that's your gracious light,
True love and teaching and the bread of life.
I know for sure that your Word will lead me on
Brighten the way all through my journey home.'[6]

Intercessory Prayer

Kefa Sempangi from Uganda shares a very painful but powerful example of how he learned a significant lesson:

'One evening at the end of a long prayer meeting, an elderly evangelist from the Revival Fellowship came to speak with me. He was a tall, thin man from the western Banyankole tribe, and he had been an evangelist for many years. "Kefa," he said, speaking in a most sober manner, "I have something to tell you. I have been listening to you pray and your prayers are not as they should be. You pray to indulge your own desires. You center on your needs or the needs of the brethren, but you do not center on Christ."

I was offended by these strong words from the evangelist and I tried to explain to him the motivation for my prayers. "Christ is the center of our needs," I said; "God has commanded us to bring all our burdens to Him."

The evangelist only shook his head. "Christ is the center of our needs," he said, "but He is first the center of our lives. Before we pray concerning our desires, we must understand God's desires and let them shape our own. Otherwise when we pray we are only reinforcing our own self-centeredness."

The message that this brother brought was a hard one to hear but as I began to understand its meaning, I joined with my brothers and sisters in a new discipline of prayer. Together we determined to make Christ the beginning and the end of all our expectations. We determined to have no hope except that which was derived from Scripture. **We**

learned that prayer was not a platform for self-expression but a self-emptying process.'[7] (emphasis added)

The Suffering Church is very aware of the power of prayer in the spiritual warfare we face daily. Dr C. Peter Wagner identifies prayer as the central foundational activity for spiritual warfare.

'In one sense prayer is a weapon of warfare and in another sense it is the medium through which all of the other weapons are utilized ... **Without prayer we are impotent in our struggle with the enemy.**'[8] (emphasis added)

Pastor Ha's church in Vietnam grew from twenty-nine to over 5,000 in just a few years during the communist regime in the late 1970s. Open Doors' President and former Vietnam missionary Johan Companjen visited him in the early 1980s and asked the secret of this phenomenal church growth.

Pastor Ha replied, 'I have a very simple theology. When you have problems, pray! When you have more problems, pray more!' Every morning this church had a well-attended prayer meeting at 6:00 a.m. And the church grew and grew. Although they were constantly living under pressure, there was one scripture text chosen for the wall of their sanctuary, *'In everything give thanks.'*

And yet after his years of imprisonment, Pastor Ha said,

'When I had my freedom, I worked with prayer sometimes in the background. In prison, I discovered that prayer is everything. It's like a pilot using a checklist before he takes off. If he skips the first item, many lives might be in danger. **The first item on our checklist should always be prayer. If we skip it, the whole mission is in jeopardy.**'[9] (emphasis added)

Vietnamese Pastor Cuong also spent over six years in prison. He says this about prayer:

'In my work I was so busy I had no time to pray. But in prison, I was thankful to God that He gave me time for prayer. I had about six hours of prayer every day.

I had time to recall every member of my congregation to pray for them (Before that I served the church but I didn't have enough time to pray for them.)

I learned about the real presence of God in prayer there. When you kneel down and pray wholeheartedly with the Lord, you feel His answer right there.' [10]

Russian poetess Irina Ratushinskaya is convinced that because of Christians around the world praying for her in the gulag, she and other prisoners experienced God's presence like 'the sense of delicious warmth in a freezing land.' [11] After her release she wrote a poem to express her gratitude to God and fellow believers. She included the words, 'My dear ones, thank you all.' [12]

Iranian martyr, Mehdi Dibaj, commented after his release from prison in early 1994,

'I thank God for keeping me safe in the prison for nine years and twenty-seven days. And I thank God for my brothers and sisters all over the world who prayed and fasted and helped me until I was released.' [13]

Prayer times together are also important to Suffering Church Christians as a fellowship factor. In his fascinating book *Siberian Miracle*, Peter de Bruijne documents the life of a significant group of believers in Chuguyevka, Siberia seeking religious freedom but also very much involved in cell group development and evangelistic outreach. He writes about them:

'Gradually the congregation settled on fixed prayer times. The first prayer would take place within the family at 6:00 in the morning, then at 10:00 a.m. and 1:00 p.m. members would pray wherever they found themselves, and finally at 7:00 in the evening family prayers would be held again. Those steady prayer times never became a fixed law, but that Soviet school of hard religious knocks had demonstrated the wisdom of developing beneficial traditions and habits while having the opportunity to do so. They said to themselves, "If persecution should come, you may not have time to think about how to stand firm. All you have to fall back on is habits of endurance and faithfulness." ' [14]

Dr Jonathan Chao of the Chinese Church Research Centre in Hong Kong shares about a house church meeting he attended in China. The believers had gathered for a special meeting in a cave twenty-five feet below ground level. After a three-hour message, 'They prayed with tears running down from their eyes, and the stream of tears intermingled with their "noserun", dripping down like transparent noodles, which they ignored. For their hearts were so turned to the face of Christ that they became totally oblivious of their own unkempt state. One sister prayed for over 45 minutes standing, pleading with the Lord to release her fellow-evangelist and fiancé from prison. He had fasted for many days and refused to divulge any information on the churches' evangelistic activity.' [15]

I'll never forget my first visit to Pastor Lamb's Chinese house church in 1985. In that dimly-lit upper room the faithful gathered an hour before service time to pray. Kneeling on bare concrete with none of our fancy kneeling pads, these Chinese Christians prayed with an intensity I had never before experienced. When one finished, several others began immediately and simultaneously. The one with the loudest voice would continue and then the same process repeated. Even though I could not understand the Chinese words, I could understand the tone and expression. The hour passed by in what seemed to be only minutes.

An itinerant evangelist in China told Dr David Wang of Asian Outreach, 'The lengthiness of our prayers is a consequence of our persecution ... For so many years we had no pastors or Bibles or even songbooks. Therefore, when we gathered together we could only pray. It became the major focus of our meetings.' [16] This comment came after an evening baptismal service that contained over five hours of prayer!

A SIM International missionary shares about returning to

Ethiopia as a water development worker under the communist regime in the 1980s. A great revival developed which he accounts for in the following statement:

> 'Prayer has been a key to revival. When the Church was underground, believers prayed every morning, at 4:00. It was prayer, I believe, that moved God and brought revival to Ethiopia. Even in their newfound freedom, Christians continue to pray. I trust they'll never lose the belief that there is power in prayer.' [17]

Prayer is also a time of listening to God as it is a time of talking to him. This is the involvement of God's Spirit. Our role is to be very sensitive to his guidance.

Two sisters in southern China came to Christ in a house church meeting. Twenty months later a friend from Hong Kong visited them and asked what they had been doing since their conversion.

'Starting home meetings,' was their timid response.

'How many home meetings?'

'Only thirty,' was their halting reply.

'How many attend your meetings?' was the next nonchalant question.

'Well, at the smallest one about two hundred and eighty!'

Now the questioner was totally involved and quickly continued, 'How many attend your largest meeting?'

'Only four thousand nine hundred!'

The Hong Kong Christian was flabbergasted. And in his excitement quickly asked, 'How do you ladies – both new Christians – know what to do?'

They simply replied, **'We pray. And after we pray, the Holy Spirit tells us what to do!'** [18] (emphasis added)

Another great example is the report from China of the Christian woman in charge of security at a coal mine. Ross Paterson shares it in his excellent volume, *Heartcry For China*:

> 'The woman suddenly felt the Holy Spirit urging her to pull the alarm lever, even though there was no apparent reason

to do so. Although everything seemed quiet and normal, she obeyed the prompting within her.

The whole mine was evacuated as a result of the alarm sounding, but when all the men had assembled on the surface, it seemed as if a huge mistake had been made. Just moments later the ground beneath their feet shook and a large section of the mine collapsed.

Because of this sister's sensitivity and willingness to obey God, everyone's lives had been saved. Additionally, however, 400 of the miners surrendered their lives to Christ after recognising that God had miraculously saved them from death.' [19]

The Chinese believers today are characterized by their oft-repeated slogan, **'Much prayer – much power; little prayer – little power.'** The early Church in the Book of Acts was a praying church. They were a people of prayer known as 'those who call on the name of the Lord.'

South Korean pastor David Cho who leads the largest church congregation in the world claims that this is also a truism in the free world when God's people commit themselves to pray. His church membership is now over 700,000 and he credits this church growth to three things: prayer, prayer, and prayer!

He shared at a National Religious Broadcasters Convention in Los Angeles that people follow their leader. Therefore, he rises at 3:30 a.m. every morning to pray. And he prays five hours per day. He adds, 'With so many church members, I cannot spend any less in prayer.'

'Prayer is the only source of power!' claims Dr Cho. 'In prayer I fellowship with God, receive His anointing, am enabled to meet life's crises, and rebuke evil powers.' He continues, 'America's pollution slide can only be stopped by massive prayer!'

He shares how one day he was in his prayer room for an hour of prayer in the afternoon when the President of South Korea phoned for his advice. His secretary refused to disturb him and the President later insisted Dr Cho fire her.

'I will not fire her,' he responded, 'She was following my

orders. I was speaking with the President of the Universe. Who is the President of South Korea?'

This church has sent out and fully supports four hundred cross-cultural missionaries.

In Acts 13, we see that the cross-cultural missionary movement began with a group of five godly, concerned men in the church at Antioch on their knees in prayer (and fasting) making themselves available to God. God spoke to them and they followed His directions and the missions movement was launched in the power of God's Spirit.

Power in Perseverance

Last summer on another visit to China I met a lovely elderly Christian lady I call Sister Alice. For over twenty-one years her husband, pastor Allen Yuan, was is prison. She was left alone with the care of their six children and her mother-in-law. The testimony she shared moved me deeply:

> 'When my husband who was a pastor was imprisoned in April 1958, I was told I would never see him again. It was a very heavy burden. I had six children and a mother-in-law to provide for. My heart was full of frustration. I argued with God about my situation. The future seemed so dark.
>
> One night God spoke to me and said, "These things have come from me!" I told Him, "If they are from You, please protect my family and me. Do not allow me to disgrace Your Name. I want to follow You and glorify You!" Then I received peace in my heart.
>
> People failed me but through those difficult years God never forsook me. But He did test me. The first test was the pressures of life. I earned only 80 cents a day. How could my family and I live on such a small income? God provided for us as he did for Elijah. He promised to be my shepherd and provider.
>
> But one night my mother-in-law announced that there was no food left for breakfast. She decided that the next morning she would go visit her daughter to request food.

That night I asked God why He had not provided for the next day. After my prayer, I heard Him say, "If I can provide for the birds, I can provide for you." I slept peacefully.

The next morning at 5:55 a.m. there was a knock at the door. I opened it to see a lady about 60 years old who I didn't know. She said, "Are you Sister Alice? It was so difficult to find you. The Spirit moved me to give you this." And she placed a parcel on the table and started to leave.

I asked her name and she replied, "I have no name. Just thank the Lord!"

She walked out and disappeared so I opened the parcel. Among some food items, it contained an envelope with $50 dollars. God is never late. We didn't even miss one meal. My mother-in-law said, "Now I don't have to visit my daughter today."

Over the months, many similar experiences occurred. People regularly sent money in the mail with no return address.

The second test was political pressure from the party. Because my husband had been arrested for refusing to submit to the Chinese government's religious policies, I was also considered to be a counter-revolutionary. I was told I would never see my husband again. Everyday authorities pressured me to criticize my religious beliefs and divorce my husband.

Everyday I was subjected to six hours of pressure in these struggle sessions. If I did not know the Lord, I would have committed suicide. Two other women I knew went insane and committed suicide under these circumstances. I hung on with the help of God. My strategy was to close my eyes and pray to endure the struggle sessions.

The third test was the pressure of work. Because of the accusations against me, I was not allowed to work in a factory or an office. Thus after the six-hour struggle sessions, I was required to do my eight hours of hard labour. I pulled wagon loads of construction bricks, stones and cement for 80 cents a day. Every load was extremely heavy.

This work made me so exhausted. I was tired out before I began. Perspiration flowed down my body. In the winter it was even more difficult to pull the wagons in the cold and over frozen mud. Sometimes I had to shovel cement over my head to the second floor. I survived by constantly praying and asking God to help me. He was merciful and gave me strength.

The fourth test was the lust of the flesh. I was 39-years-old when my husband was taken. The government officials tried to persuade me to marry another man. If only I would submit to the officials, I would be permitted to move into new living quarters. My records would all be changed to look brand new and I would no longer have to bear the heavy burdens.

Some men came to me with gifts of money and clothes and one even prepared a divorce declaration for me. They'd quietly knock at my door at midnight.

I'd tell them, "I'm a Christian. I cannot divorce or remarry." God loved me so much He gave me the strength to overcome all these temptations for a comfortable life. Whenever I prayed, He provided all that I needed ... even more abundantly than I had asked.

After twenty-one years and eight months my husband was released from prison. Over twenty-one years of separation is a long time. But God led us through.'[20]

If the disciplines of spiritual warfare are the Word and prayer, the central attitude for those in the battle is faithful obedience. In order to continuously walk in the Spirit and produce the fruit of the Spirit, we must have that quality which we call perseverance.

In Romans 5:3, the Apostle Paul says it is suffering that produces perseverance which in turn produces character. And in Revelation 3:10, Jesus commends the church in Philadelphia because they kept his command to endure patiently – that is, persevere. It is not a call to just 'hang in there' and do nothing, 'but to work deliberately, knowing with certainty that God will never be defeated.'[21]

The enemy's attempt to counter this quality is to create spiritual battle fatigue followed by spiritual lethargy – a general attitude we simply call giving up!

John Bunyon described it in *Pilgrims Progress* as the 'Enchanted Ground' near the end of the journey where unwary pilgrims simply fall asleep and never wake to finish their journey.

A frail sister in China who was severely persecuted commented, **'A ship cannot stop just because there is a storm. It just has to make sure it stays on the right course. Without times like these, we may not know how to serve the Lord.'**

For me there is nothing more enjoyable than being on a ship at sea during good weather. My fondest memories are from the months of Project Pearl – the delivery of one million Chinese Bibles on June 18, 1981. I will never forget the warm wind blowing my beard and the fresh ocean smell while standing on the bow of Tugboat Michael early in the morning as the sun rose over the eastern horizon. The porpoises playfully led the way and multitudes of flying fish skimmed on the surface of the deep blue ocean that was as calm and smooth as a mirror.

There was also nothing more terrifying for me than being 'stuck' on Tugboat Michael in what seemed to be the middle of nowhere during a terrible long storm. There was nowhere to go to avoid its effects as the ship noisily crashed into huge waves and rolled madly from side to side. There was no way to get off. We just had to pray and ride it out.

Life is also like that. During those terrible storms the Suffering Church testify that all you can do is lash yourself to the helm and hold fast to your confidence in God's faithfulness and His everlasting love in Christ Jesus.

Hebrews 10:19–39 is a great passage to study on this topic. The key verse for me is verse 36:

> *'You need to persevere so that when you have done the will of God, you will receive what he has promised.'*

The interesting thing to note is that this verse stands in the context of suffering insults and persecution, imprisonment and property confiscation.

Open Doors co-worker Jeff Taylor was visiting a pastor in Cuba who was experiencing severe hardship and difficulties. He asked him, 'With all these problems, don't you ever want to give up?' The pastor smiled and simply replied, **'If there were no battles, there would be no victory!'** Someone else once said, 'Whatever does not kill me, strengthens me.'

The Chinese people would not have had the Bible in their language as early as they did without this quality in the lives of pioneer missionaries. Robert Morrison grew up in a poverty-stricken area of a Scotland manufacturing town. A Sunday School teacher did not give up on him and after much perseverance by that teacher, young Morrison became a follower of Jesus.

He went on to become the Protestant pioneer missionary who translated the Bible into the Chinese language in the early 1800s. But not without many trying difficulties. It took him sixteen years under terrible working conditions. His Chinese assistant, Ako, carried poison to take as suicide rather than endure the treatment he knew he would receive if discovered. Later he was rewarded by Ako becoming his first convert.

Robert Morrison lost his son and then his wife. But he persevered. Today his gravestone beside his wife's and son's can be visited in the old Protestant cemetery in Macao. A monument to the multi-linked chain of godly perseverance.

That chain continues today through the lives of many brothers and sisters in China.

Dorothy Ai Ching now travels North America sharing how her twenty years in a terrible labour camp in China where she spent her energies shovelling manure made her fit for the Master's use. She now concludes that her first lesson learned from her experiences was that God honours perseverance.[22]

Another Chinese believer wrote to a Christian radio program producer in Hong Kong about the persecution his teenage son was receiving for his Christian faith. He concludes, 'I told him,

"The way of the Cross is difficult, but we must persevere on this road of eternal life." ' [23]

J.J. Andrews is an elderly Lutheran pastor friend in Rangoon, Burma – now Myanmar – with a great heart for ministry. Several years ago his daughter died of viral hepatitis. Two months later his wife passed away from a broken heart. Six months after that one of his sons suddenly died. He was crushed. He said, 'I felt like Job, only no one visited me.'

A young Filipino staff member of Open Doors in Bangkok, Thailand, Ver Enriquez heard about this situation. He made a special trip just to visit Brother J.J. and encourage him. J.J. said, 'Thank you for coming in my darkest hour.'

Some months later, I was visiting Brother J.J. in Rangoon. He had his young grand-children laughing and playing around his home. He smiled as he shared unforgettable lessons with me. The words I remember verbatim were, **'God rewarded me for my perseverance and healed my broken heart!'**

On our first visit to London, England, my family and I stayed in a Christian bed-and-breakfast home in Putney. Mrs Worsley had a plaque on the wall of her dining room that was so dominant in decor and poignant in message that we read it aloud every morning and discussed it during each breakfast. It read:

> **'Sometimes the Lord calms the storm.**
> **Sometimes he lets the storm rage...**
>   **and quiets his child.'**

Lord, you have asked me to take advantage of your armour to stand strong in the spiritual battles I face every day. Forgive me for my lack of mastery of your Word and for my prayerlessness. Help me to patiently persevere in my service for you. And thank you for your promise that in your strength I can be victorious.

*We don't go to church
we are the church!*

Ernest Southcott

Secret Six —
All in the family

Jesus Christ calls his followers to be the church — not play church. Our passion for him is to be followed by our passion for the family of God. As the church, we are to fulfil the functions of evangelism, discipleship, fellowship and worship.

Chapter 6

All In the Family

Daniel sat in the chair still shaking his head in unbelief. As an overseas Chinese, he had just returned from his first extensive visit to the People's Republic of China. Now in the freedom of his home city, Singapore, he was trying to assimilate and communicate all the impressions and messages he had received.

'How would you summarize what you learned on your visit, Daniel?' I asked.

He continued to just shake his head and smile. Finally he began to verbally respond.

'Probably by the visit to one particular house church,' he slowly replied. 'It numbers several hundred believers who experienced a severe degree of persecution over the past years. I asked them how they had been able to survive and even grow during such terrible experiences.

'They very quickly replied with three points,' he continued. **'First, obedience to the Word of God. Second, communication with God: prayer. And third, love for the brothers and sisters.'**

As I have studied the stories and reports of other persecuted Christian groups in several countries, I have seen and heard the same conclusions. First comes the passion of our relationship with God and then the passion of our relationship with brothers and sisters in God's family.

In the late 1970s Dr Everett Boyce, a missionary with Open Doors at the time, did considerable research on the church under restriction – especially in Asia. He received significant input from Rev. Walter Routh Jr who spent many years with his family as a missionary in Vietnam until the fall of Saigon in 1975.

Based on his study of the Scriptures with the witness in practical experience of the Suffering Church, Dr Boyce concluded that there are only three requirements for a church: personal faith in Jesus Christ as Lord and Saviour; two or more individuals sharing faith in Christ; commitment to Christ and then to each other.[1]

Once a church exists, there are then just four basic functions of the church: **evangelize**, **disciple**, **fellowship** and **worship**.[2] This simplicity is what has made the church of Jesus Christ such a living, growing organism since he instituted it. Nowhere is this more obvious than among our family who make up the body we call the Suffering Church. And nowhere in modern times have we seen revival and church growth to the extent they have. They are not dependent on physical forms and traditional methods. With only these four functions any group of believers, established by God, can survive victoriously – and even grow – in the most hostile environment.

David Adenay, a noted China watcher, now with the Lord, was known for often saying that the simplicity of the church in China was articulated in 'the three loves': love for Jesus; love for one another; love for the lost.

It always seems necessary in the western world to point out that the 'church' is not a reference to a building. I have appreciated the evangelical Christians in Russia and Ukraine. There the worship centers are referred to as a **'House of Prayer'** not a church. In Cuba, the worship centers are referred to as the **'Templo'**. These believers are more aware than we that the church is only made up of people – and not with the buildings in which they meet. Serious problems can arise when Christians are confused on this point.

Before the fall of Saigon, some Vietnamese church leaders thought that their lack of funds for buildings and complex programs was the cause of the slow growth of Christianity there. On one occasion, the following conversation was overheard:

'Do you have Communists in your part of the country?' the observer asked.

'Most assuredly. They are there,' the church leader replied.

'Are they growing in numbers and influence?' he then asked.

The leader hesitated momentarily, then admitted sadly, 'Yes, they are growing very fast.'

'Can you show me their meeting places, and schools or introduce me to their leaders?' the observer continued.

'Certainly not,' the leader said in disgust. 'If they are known, they will be arrested.'

'You mean they are secret, without buildings or property and still they grow in number?' the observer asked in amazement.

'Yes, you could say that,' the leader responded.

'Then it must be that their growing influence does not depend on such things. If they can be wrong in their beliefs and still grow without money and buildings, why do you think the church of Jesus Christ needs them?'[3]

The lesson was quickly learned. Today the house church movement in Vietnam is growing as significantly and quickly as in neighbouring China.

It is very interesting that the early church had none of these things yet according to Acts 17:6 turned their world upside down!

Chinese pastor Allen Yuan tells his frequent visitors, **'If you want to know how to establish a church, read the book of Acts one hundred times!'**

Evangelism

Eight men sat in a small dimly lit room in a rural Chinese village home. Seven were preachers and their eyes were glued to the Bible held by the eighth man. It was a leather-bound zippered Bible with gold-edged trim on the pages.

John, the Open Doors researcher, suddenly became aware

that the seven men were staring intently at his Bible. One of them generated enough courage to say, 'What a beautiful Bible. May I look at it for a moment?'

'Of course,' replied John. The Bible was gently handed from person to person as though it was made of eggshells. They asked how much it cost. And their faces fell when they learned it was the equivalent of twenty dollars.

Then John received an inspiration. He decided to make this a personal ministry project. The qualification for receiving one of these Chinese Bibles should be so high that these leaders would be inspired to greater achievement. Yet, at the same time ensure that he would not need to provide a great number.

He told them, 'If a person is mightily used by God, then I will bring him one of these Bibles.'

'What do you mean, mightily used of God?', the preachers queried eagerly.

Thinking fast John said, 'Those who have led at least 10,000 people to the Lord and discipled another 10,000.'

To his astonishment the preachers burst out laughing. They said, 'Oh, this is too easy. There are five of us here who can now qualify for your zippered gold-edged Bible, and we know ten more.'

After his trip John chuckled, 'I'm bankrupt.' But more seriously he added, 'I've been working in China with house church leaders for many years. But one thing never changes . . . I am literally taken by surprise during each visit at how fast the church is growing.' [4]

Evangelism is the natural outreach of a body of believers who love God and love each other. And for most members of the Suffering Church, evangelism is the one factor that can add to their persecution or pressures. Yet they display some of the most creative methods in sharing Christ despite their restrictions.

Elderly Aunty Esther in China has a favourite witnessing method. She boards a local city bus at its terminus where she is sure to get a seat. During its run with people crowded inside, Aunty Esther reads aloud stories about Jesus from her Bible. If anyone shows interest, she hands them a slip of paper with her address and an invitation to come to her home and talk.

Aunty Esther does not fear the authorities who treated this kind of activity with severity. She is often quoted as saying, 'At my age and after all I've suffered, what can they do to me now?' She shared with me on one visit that her strategies for personal evangelism had helped her lead dozens of people to Jesus including some people very high placed in the Chinese government and media circles. She is also prepared for the discipling that follows.

Tony Lambert shares about his observing the remarkable open-air witness for the Lord in the heart of China's capital – on Tiananmen Square in May of 1989:

'But then I heard a new note: the sound of hymn-singing. Amidst the sea of banners coming into view in front of the Great Hall of the People, the sign of the cross was lifted high. The white banner with a large red cross proclaimed in Chinese characters "God so loved the world". I pushed through the crowd to investigate. About twenty students, all Christians, were clustered round the banner. Their leader held high a small wooden cross. They sang heartily, "I am a true soldier of Christ". Then with dozens of curious spectators holding up tape recorders to catch this unique event, they launched into "Rock of Ages". I joined in.' [5]

Two weeks later thousands of students who demonstrated on that square were dead – including some of these Christians.

In neighbouring Vietnam, a young Christian mother involved in the house church movement was taken to the police station at night for interrogation. Her husband was already in prison for evangelizing. As she prayed, the Lord gave her new boldness. She told her persecutors, 'If you stop my brothers from preaching the Word, others will preach in their place. If you send them to jail, they will preach there. We will not stop until all 68 million citizens of Vietnam are saved.' [6]

Vietnamese house church Pastor Ai told me, **'God gives everyone their own special way to witness for him.'** He has a member who drives a bus and is responsible for it on the weekends. The driver is able to get permission to drive the bus to the beach on Sundays for an outing with different members of the community. Of course, he invites his unsaved neighbours.

The trip takes over two hours and all the way there Pastor Ai has a 'captive audience' for sharing the gospel. He reports that by the time they reach the beach, there are many new candidates for water baptism. This pastor estimates that over five hundred people have come to Christ through this creative method.

Open Doors colleague Hector Tamez often shares the testimony of Manuel in Peru. He was an effective evangelist among the mountain Quechua people. One day the Shining Path guerrillas stopped him on the trail and told him to stop going to the mountains, stop handing out Bibles, cassettes and other Christian materials, and stop preaching about Jesus. They threatened his life.

Some weeks later Manuel's dead body was found on the trail. His feet, hands and tongue had been cut off. With a knife they carved on his torso the message, 'We told you to stop!' The chopped body parts completed the message – " ... visiting the villages, distributing Bibles, preaching about Jesus!'

At his memorial service, 25 young people committed themselves to take the place of Manuel. A wise old man asked these idealistic youths if they were prepared for the same demise as Manuel's. One young man cried out, 'If we die, a thousand others will rise to take our places!'

Sudan in Africa is a country where Christians are being severely persecuted with little knowledge about it in the West. Many Christians have died for their faith – some even crucified. Wybo, an Open Doors researcher, was visiting in the Sudan and was amazed to hear Christians greeting one another. After the normal first two questions about the other person's welfare and family, the third question was, 'How many have you led to Christ in the past fourteen days?' Because there was a positive answer each time, the fourth question was 'What are you doing to disciple them?' The fifth question then logically followed, 'How many have they been leading to the Lord?'

Colleagues working in China encountered one house church that grew by 15,000 new believers just in the first half of 1994. They also shared about a Chinese sister who was in prison with over 4,000 other inmates. After a short time there were over five hundred new believers. A Chinese pastor's wife was very sick in bed. But she was rejoicing that she had led more people to Christ in four months being bed-ridden than in her forty years of ministry.

The most remarkable story from China is about a Christian lady in prison during the 'anti-spiritual pollution campaign' in the mid-eighties. She spent her time hand carving Scripture verses in miniature lettering with a sharpened end of a tooth-brush on the walls and even the frame of the cot in her cell. Years later she actually met another person who later spent time in the same cell and came to Christ through reading those verses over and over.

Two summers ago when visiting Christians in the north of China, I asked the whereabouts of Aunty Mabel. This short octo-genarian medical doctor, I was told, was away on a missions outreach in spiritually needy Tibet. Last summer she was home and very anxious to hear of our group experience in Tibet – the rooftop of the world – since she was planning another mission trip soon. She concluded, **'Jesus is saying, "Hurry up and get the job done so I can come back again!"'** [7]

Tony Lambert remembers meeting a group of Christian Chinese in Shanghai in 1990. They already had begun training young Christians for world evangelism.[8] They share an opti-mism that God will soon answer their prayer as articulated in Psalm 67:2,

> *'Send us around the world with the news of your saving power and your eternal plan for all mankind.'*   [Living Bible]

As I write, a report arrives from a visit to China of a US Congressional delegation headed by Congressman Chris Smith of New Jersey. Although the trip was political, the team members were enthralled by the spiritual messages received – a new chapter of Acts written throughout China.

In Karen Feaver's report of the trip, she shares about the impact of a Christian woman who was released from her second prison term:

'During her 110 days in captivity, she was hung upside down and beaten with electrical cords ... Like the martyrs from the early church, she said that God's presence was so tangible during the torture that, in fact, she felt joyful. "Because of these afflictions, we loved the souls of China more," she said, "And we prayed for those who were torturing us"...

"The local regulations are against the Word of God," one of the younger women explained, "so we ignore them and have been travelling in groups of 10 to 20 to share the gospel since the early 1980s. **The only way the church can survive is through evangelism.**' Congressmen do not normally take notes for themselves, but Chris Smith picked up his pen to record personally their daily battle cry: "We go out ready to preach the gospel, ready to go to jail, and ready to die for Jesus' sake."...

One house-church leader described the great spiritual hunger among the young that followed Tiananmen Square. A young Christian businessman told us of leading 70 percent of his workers to Christ in a matter of months. The women spoke of 40,000 coming to Christ during one recent month of 'gospel sharing'.

They also asked that we pray for freedom so they could travel openly to preach the gospel throughout China, in America, and then "all the way back to Jerusalem to **finish** the task".'[9] (emphasis added)

Kefa Sempangi from Uganda sums it up well,

'We began to understand that evangelism was not a program or a method, but a life-style of submission and service to others.'[10]

Discipleship

Nora's words were all tumbling out at once and I could hardly understand her. Her scandinavian blue eyes were large and dancing with as much excitement as her speech.

'You'll, never guess what happened!' she blurted out.

'Nora, it's lunch time. Let's go to a noodle stall across the street and you can tell me the whole story.'

We set off in the Singapore heat to the food stall on the corner. There, perched on little stools with chopsticks in hand, we relived the exhilaration of Nora's first courier trip to China.

'I was able to go back to the "hard seat" cars on the train,' she continued, 'and I met a Chinese Christian gal who spoke English.'

Nora bubbled as she went on to share how together they spent the whole night witnessing to other Chinese young people on the train. By arrival time, there were two more members in the kingdom of God.

She went directly to the home of Aunty Esther where she was to leave her load of Chinese Bibles which God had enabled her to get through customs successfully.

Diminutive Aunty Esther welcomed Nora warmly with her large smile and 'Praise the Lord!' She was especially excited to see the big bag of Bibles since her supply had recently been exhausted.

'Please excuse me for a few moments,' she said to Nora, 'because I'm discipling a young lady who just received the Lord a few days ago. She works for the Beijing Daily News and has no Bible. Now I can give her one of these you brought.'

Nora was happy to wait for what turned out to be about an hour. Then she spent time in prayer and fellowship with this elderly Chinese saint who has a perpetual overflow of joy. Aunty Esther shared how her supply of Bibles was depleted quickly because of the great demand for God's Word. There were always new Christians on her 'waiting list'.

Since the next day was Sunday, Nora asked for directions to the Three Self Protestant Church in the city where she could observe a Chinese worship service.

Nora's train companion attended with her to interpret what turned out to be a very evangelistic and biblically sound message. After the sermon, three people went to the front altar to pray. As Nora and her companion were about to leave, a group of young Australian tourists approached her with a problem.

'We heard that Bibles were badly needed here in China,' they started, 'so we went to the Bible Society in Australia and bought a bagful. But when we came to this church today, one of the pastors told us they don't need any more Bibles here. They now print their own. And they wouldn't accept our gift! Do you know what we can do with them?'

Nora grinned broadly as she wiped a perspiration bead from her cheek, finished chewing a mouthful of noodles and continued.

'I gladly rescued them from their quandary,' she beamed, 'and put the bag on my shoulder to leave.

'But just then the three people who had been praying at the front were coming back up the aisle. And to my surprise one was Aunty Esther and another was the new believer she had been discipling the day before.'

Aunty Esther ran to Nora and excitedly shared that the third person was the young lady's fiancé who had just prayed the sinners prayer at the altar and committed his life to Jesus. Then her beaming face turned solemn.

'But I've already distributed all the Bibles you brought yesterday. I've none left for this young man.'

Nora placed Aunty Esther's hand on her bulging shoulder bag. 'God has provided – again!'

Christians in China have often reminded me that Jesus' Great Commission was to **make disciples**.[11] They feel that Western Christians have paraphrased Matthew 28:18 to say 'As you go into all the world, **make believers . . .** '

The key element in discipling new believers is the Bible. Without the authoritative Word of God, on what foundation do you learn and with what curriculum do you teach and train? The group Daniel met in China (in the beginning of this chapter) discipled themselves by memorizing as a body one chapter per week from the Bible.

This is why Open Doors is so strong on providing God's Word to those who are cut off from access to it. Although Open Doors is just as involved in encouragement and actual on-site leadership training, Bible delivery has become our best known suit. It is amazing – even in a post-Iron Curtain era – to learn of the many locations where our brothers and sisters do not have adequate copies of the Bible or even parts of it. Interestingly, it is most often these same locations where the church is growing the fastest.

In these areas, it is also significant that the body of Christ is noted for its philosophy, 'Every Home A Church'. **When focus is taken off the building – whether by force or voluntarily – one's spiritual life becomes centred around and based on the family.** Since meetings generally have to be held in a home, the head of the household becomes responsible for the spiritual care and growth of the individuals gathering under his roof. Sometimes this is just one extended family. Indeed the family is a microcosm of the universal church.

The children of Christian families in these areas and situations seem to be under special attack by Satan. I am greatly impacted by Christian parents in the former Soviet Union who spend days every week praying and fasting for their children's salvation and spiritual growth. It challenges me too that at the end of services I attend in a 'House of Prayer', the pastor often reminds the worshippers 'Remember to pray for our children.'

The house church movement in China developed in response to tremendous pressure over the years by the authorities on institutional churches. Most analysts of China's church history consider this development one of the main reasons for its survival and growth. It has generated a flexibility and purity that greatly challenge our traditions.

Earlier I mentioned Walter Routh Jr, an American missionary to South Vietnam before the fall of Saigon in 1975. Years before the ultimate collapse of the regime in the South, Walter saw it coming. Thus he concentrated his efforts on planting and developing house churches (some prefer to call them cell groups). After being forced to leave, he monitored these Vietnamese house churches from the Philippines and was very encouraged to learn of their strength, growth and longevity under the communist regime's pressures.

The de-institutionalizing of the church in creative-access countries has actually been liberating for them. In China, Vietnam and Cuba, I have heard house church leaders share how current events in their group was an additional chapter to the Book of Acts.

Some even adopt communal living based on the early church model in the book of Acts of holding all things in common – especially in a communist setting. The Christian community in Chuguyevka, Far East Russia exemplified the fact that any good idea that Marx may have had was only practical in a truly Christian life style:

> 'Yet the people from the community never promoted their particular lifestyle. Just as in Central Asia, they refrained from pushing their ideas of living together like the early Christians did. Curious people were always welcome to join for a time. Some did and stayed, although most of them found it impossible to change their own lives that much.
>
> But joining wasn't necessary for everybody, as the Chuguyevka pentecostals often said, "Living as we do is not the only way of being a Christian. God is much larger than the lives we are able to show" ...
>
> Nikolai Vins said: "If you proclaim the Gospel and establish a congregation, you must be able to say, 'Come, have a look at how Christians live.' That's the most powerful recommendation. Our first goal is to strengthen solitary Christians and help them be a good example in their own environment. First be a light yourself, and then help others to be a light, and after that still others will be attracted to turn towards God also." ' [12]

I am not trying to present a case for the demise of the institutional church. I, myself, am a product of the same and a supporter of it. But there are certainly benefits and advantages to consider from house fellowships – especially in the area of discipling followers of Jesus. We need to find a biblical balance.

Fellowship

Rene looked carefully both ways as he turned the corner. No one seemed to be watching. Wiping the perspiration from his forehead he glanced at his watch. He was five minutes early. He walked slowly around the block a second time to arrive at the large gate at exactly 7:14. He pressed the bell three times: short ... long ... short. It was the newly changed code to indicate he was a fellow-believer. The gate opened and closed quickly as Rene slipped inside. In two hours time there were several hundred believers gathered secretly in the basement for fellowship.

Rene sat quietly waiting for the others. He smiled with approval as his eyes scanned the array of musical instruments on stands beside the big drum set. Through one side door, he could see the huge library of Christian books and tapes. In the far corner he noticed a new addition – a photocopier. It sat beside the well-used high speed tape duplicators. And everywhere he looked was further evidence of the extensive soundproofing.

He remembered reading in an Open Doors magazine about a small group in China that gathered weekly in the back room of a small store to worship together. It was the era of the infamous cultural revolution. Since the believers could easily be overheard by anyone entering the store, they 'sang' hymns together without words or music. Someone whispered the name of the song and they would silently move their lips and simply think of the words and music.

He chuckled out loud. The memory came of Pastor Wally saying, 'We are an underground Church like the believers behind the Bamboo Curtain, but the difference is that we can praise in full voice because the facilities are sound proofed. Not even our closest neighbour can hear us.' [13]

This is a description of a church group in Riyadh, Saudi Arabia – a country that has not had an official church in over fourteen hundred years. And yet many believers meet together secretly and at great risk all over the country.

In fact in much of our world even today, Christians

deliberately take extraordinary risks by meeting in secret for fellowship. A recent article in *The Toronto Star* newspaper was headlined, **'Christians in Somalia Must Worship in Secret'**. The article quoted a source as saying, 'Just being openly Christian is now enough to get yourself killed here.'[14]

The reason for believers taking this risk is wrapped up in the significant word **encouragement**. Hebrews 10:25 indicates that an important reason for regularly meeting together is even beyond the aspect of communal worship; namely, encouraging one another. And we are to do it even more as we see the Lord's return coming closer.

Some use the term 'serving' as a contemporary synonym for this concept. Because serving is essentially responding generously to other people's needs – thus encouraging them. But encouragement has a subtle nuance that goes beyond the concept and motivation of serving others.

During the difficult times in Romania, a young believer was called in to the secret police for interrogation. He had dreaded this moment. Fear gripped him throughout, and he was unable to give a categoric answer rejecting the police offers of good prospects and security, if he would inform on his fellow-believers.

He did not accept the offer, but his inability to reject it unquestioningly brought personal agony. He could not sleep that night, trembling from fear and guilt.

The next morning, led by the Spirit of God, an older Christian came to visit the family. He was unaware of the young man's dilemma, but being a former prisoner for the faith himself, he was able to discern and give counsel from Scripture to the young man.

He built up the young man in fellowship, training him for the next interrogation ordeal. That came the next afternoon. The young man was still upset about his answers the second time; and again the older believer came to encourage him.

Three days passed in this fashion. Eventually the young man was able to reject the police offer completely. He was let go. Discernment, counsel, prayer and patient caring had brought him through and trained him in righteousness.[15]

Encouragement, as fellowship, requires time spent together. It's the act of inspiring others with renewed courage, spirit or hope. And in humility each of us must come to the point where we acknowledge we need massive doses of it regularly.

Chuck Swindoll points out that the root word for encouragement in Hebrews 10:25 is the same as describing the Holy Spirit in John fourteen and sixteen. He concludes,

> 'In fact, when we encourage others, we come as close to the work of the Holy Spirit as anything we can do in God's family.' [16]

The great Greek scholar, Dr William Barclay, also concludes,

> 'One of the highest of human duties is the duty of encouragement ... It is easy to pour cold water on their enthusiasm; it is easy to discourage others. The world is full of discouragers. We have a Christian duty to encourage one another. Many a time a word of praise or thanks or appreciation or cheer has kept a man on his feet.' [17]

This fellowship of Christian brothers and sisters thus takes on the character of encouragement. But it is also intimate and relational. I have always been impressed that Jesus chose only twelve out of his many followers to be **'with him'**. To be with him involves our time, affections, interests and desires.

Brother Andrew learned early in his ministry the importance of encouragement when he fellowshipped with Christians in restricted situations in Eastern Europe. They told him, 'Andrew, just your being here is worth ten of your best sermons!' Today as he travels in the Muslim dominated world, he receives the same comment. Indeed, he often defines the generic ministry of Open Doors as encouragement – which is expanded by returning for further fellowship and providing requested material or training assistance.

Some Open Doors couriers visited a pastor in the southern part of Vietnam. They could not speak Vietnamese and he was very suspicious of them. So they did what the Spirit prompted.

They knelt on the floor of the sanctuary and began to pray out loud in English. Soon the pastor joined them with tears flowing down his face. That pastor later wrote them a letter as to the importance of their visit which was translated as follows:

> 'It was deeply moving that you and I could pray and praise the name of Jesus together. Although we have different languages, we can understand each other in the love of the Lord and through the Holy Spirit.
>
> We know that you want to give our church the Bible. We praise the Lord that He revealed our need to you ... and He will help you bring the Bibles in. We have told Him about this need and we are awaiting His answer.'

The areas of fellowship and encouragement repeatedly came up in my researching of Christians in prison. How joyful their reports of meeting another brother or sister in the prison or camp. And absolute rapture when the two – or more – could spend time together.

Valentina Saveleva spent five years in the harsh Soviet camps because of transporting Christian literature. She found the camp very depressing and shares how God answered her prayers:

> 'The Lord saw my need and in his mercy sent me a Christian sister named Natasha ... The Lord sent her to give me relief in my critical moment of need. We prayed together a lot and always tried to support one another in the arms of prayer. I remember how we often met outside at night under the open heavens. We couldn't stay there long, because the temperature was often below $-40°$ Fahrenheit and our work boots didn't keep our feet very warm. We would sing and pray for a few minutes, go back to our separate barracks to warm up a little, then meet outside again. Sometimes we stood silently, just gazing together toward heaven...
>
> Sometimes my only desire was that the Lord would hurry up and take me home to be with him. But Natasha refreshed me very much. She had such a solid influence for

good on my life. Often I thought that the Lord sent her to that camp just for my sake.' [18]

Richard Wurmbrand tells the story of eighteen elderly men confined in a Bucharest prison. It was

'a windowless underground room with water dripping from the roof. To avoid freezing to death, the men formed themselves into a human snake, each one clinging to the man in front for warmth, as they stamped around in an endless circle. Often a man collapsed, but the others always dragged him up from the water and forced him on. Warmth and encouragement and life – all this we gain from one another.' [19]

Worship

Ugandan pastor Kefa Sempangi shares that under the intense persecution of Idi Amin, the Holy Spirit united the hearts of Uganda's church leaders. The emphasis became loving one another and rejecting the earlier focus on differences. He writes,

'But now we heard God's call to live broken lives before one another. We were not to build our fellowship on the foundation of baptism, tongues or liturgy. We were to build on the reconciling blood of Jesus Christ.' [20]

I have already mentioned repeatedly the significance of the house church movement around the world and especially among the Suffering Church. This informal structure has the most flexibility in allowing believers to worship the Lord together. When God is truly worshipped, then discipleship, fellowship and evangelism will be a natural outcome.

Wherever Christians are restricted in practising their faith, the experience of meeting corporately for worship seems to have much more intensity and meaning. After – or sometimes before – a long hard day of work in an anti-spiritual environment, they are most desirous of meeting with the family of God to express their love, adoration and praise to their Lord.

Even where the institutional church is strong, this kind of persecution or pressure brings about a unity that honours God. Burma is the model to which I was first exposed. Missionaries were all expelled in 1966. My first visit was in the early seventies. The church was a small minority in a dominant Buddhist society with a secular socialist government.

On Sunday, I was asked to speak and break bread with the Brethren believers, in the afternoon share with the Baptists and in the evening speak at the Pentecostal church. No one asked me my denomination. I was simply a 'Brother in Christ' and represented an evangelical organization, the Far East Broadcasting Company.

I found this unity so refreshing. And, praise the Lord, I have discovered it in other parts of our world, most often outside of North America. The closest geographic location is on the island of Cuba. What a joy to be with Baptist and Pentecostal pastors together who regularly spend hours on their knees before God with one another. How refreshing to attend youth evangelism meetings with a variety of denominations present in the audience and speakers. Is there any wonder why revival is sweeping the island today?

Dr John Pitt, Open Doors' Director for Africa for many years, shares how the infamous dictator of Uganda, Idi Amin, banned twenty-seven Christian denominations and sects in September of 1977.

'Within days of the ban, thousands of secret house fellowships had sprung up across the land. Baptists, Pentecostals and other denominations organized themselves so they could meet secretly in homes or in the forests.

One of the most amazing organizers of the Secret Church in Uganda was Ben Oluka, who became "God's double agent" in the President's office. He often used his access to secret documents to tip off believers who were about to be arrested. Even more dangerous, Oluka actually pastored a house fellowship in his own home. It was a small group from the Deliverance Church, an indigenous Ugandan evangelical fellowship.

Oluka says, "At the time, I was working in the office that had to enforce the President's ban, and secretly I was running a secret church myself.

"When the ban was announced, house meetings sprang up throughout the country. There is a higher power, and when government restricts the freedom of worship, God's supremacy has to take over.

"The free churches decided to follow the example of Acts 20:20, where the believers went from house to house breaking bread and worshipping God." ' [21]

And where this model is followed, there seems to be an openness to the move of God's Spirit. Open Doors-Asia received the following letter in 1985 from five Chinese Christian young people in the south of China:

'We went to Henan province to visit a house church there. Wherever we went, we felt that we were in the time of the apostles – filled with the Spirit, excited and on fire. Signs and wonders also followed us and confirmed what we preached. Therefore many people came to the Lord.

In those villages alone, more than ninety-five per cent of the peasants have come to the Lord. The minimum attendance at each meeting point is 400–500 people. Big meetings will have more than 1,700. All are held in the open air no matter if it rains or shines. We were so amazed to see their love for the Lord.

Their meeting time is from 6:00 to 8:00 a.m. Their houses are widely scattered. Some live ten to twenty miles away from the meeting place where it takes more than three hours to walk. Their incomes are very low and they don't have bicycles. Every morning they wake up between 3:00 and 4:00 a.m. and quickly walk to the meeting place. They love to sing praises to the Lord. It is really wonderful to see how on fire for the Lord they are!' [22]

Dr David Wang shares how he once preached to about seventy young people at a house church meeting in a remote part of northwest China:

> 'To start, I took about three hours and preached on the "Lord's Prayer". The young people were squatting and sitting all over the mud floor or leaning against the wall of that little hut. They were not just listening. They were writing down every word I spoke.
>
> After I finished, the house church leader gave me some tea, saying, "Please have some tea. And then you can preach to us again." Now that was after three hours of solid preaching! I took my tea and I preached for another four hours. All this time these young people were taking down notes and echoing "Amen, amen." Finally I sat down, totally exhausted. The house church leader said, "Now let us sing." So they began to sing. And I was shocked as I listened to them singing. The first few sentences went like this:

> > "Don't listen to sermons, don't listen to sermons.
> > We will not listen to sermons..."

> Now after almost seven hours of listening to sermons they sang, "Don't listen to sermons!" Then they gave the answer. Clenching their fists, they sang, **"We will live out the sermons!"** [23] (emphasis added)

Dr J.I. Packer says,

> '...Taking the Holy Spirit seriously means that Christians must re-discover the naturalness of three things that modern believers in the West rarely see as natural – namely, **worship, evangelism and suffering.'** [24] (emphasis added)

In the sixteenth century, Teresa of Avila penned the significant words:

'God of love, help us remember
that Christ has no body now on earth but ours,
no hands but ours, no feet but ours.
Ours are the eyes to see the needs of the world.
Ours are the hands with which to bless everyone now.
Ours are the feet with which he is to go about doing
   good.'[25]

Lord, you have asked me to also have a passion for
my brothers and sisters who make up your worldwide church. Forgive me for my lack of concern and
involvement. Please help me to be part of a body
that fulfils your design and functions for the church
– especially in my own family. Thank you for your
suffering church that exhibits these principles so
clearly.

*Love is the greatest thing
that God can give us;
for [he] himself is love:
and it is the greatest thing
we can give to God.*

Jeremy Taylor

Secret Seven –
The full circle of love

Absolutely nothing can separate us from the love of God that is in Christ Jesus our Lord! Therefore, love him with all your being.

Chapter 7

Inseparable Love

There was a sick feeling in my stomach as I stood in the long customs lines at the old Saigon Thon Son Nut airport. It was 1984 and I was back in Vietnam for the first time under the communist regime.

The customs officers were thoroughly searching everyone's suitcases and carry-on bags. In my bags were numerous Vietnamese Scriptures. And the words from our briefing echoed in my head:

'Whatever happens, don't let them see the tribal Christian literature. They consider the tribal people to be connected with the CIA.'

'Lord,' I prayed. 'This looks like an impossible situation!' In the tension of the moment, I forgot that God specializes in impossible situations.

My mind relived the easy and friendly entries I had made in this same airport during the Vietnam War as I supervised Vietnamese program origination for the Far East Broadcasting Company in Manila, Philippines. The customs personnel now looked very grim. And you could see tension etched in the faces of all those waiting in the lengthy lines.

During the long wait, my mind also recalled the report of the last group of Christian couriers who had come to Vietnam. They found themselves in a line behind a lady from France who wore a large floppy hat and carried a cage with a cat in it.

When she was examined, she had no quarantine papers for the cat. This delayed her processing considerably until our colleagues were literally the last ones left in the customs hall. They were very concerned about their large and heavy bags loaded with Vietnamese Bibles.

When they came to the customs desk, the officers said, 'We're so sorry this lady and her cat kept you waiting! Please take your bags and go right through!'

I looked around the room for a lady with a floppy hat and a cat – but none was in sight.

Finally, it was my turn. I nervously handed my passport and customs papers to the lady officer. Like the others ahead of me she asked me to count my money in front of her.

Just as I was nearly finished, she stopped me abruptly with the clear English words, 'Sir, you did not declare your rings!'

I was very surprised. 'I've never had to declare my rings – anywhere!' I countered.

'You must declare your rings here. How much are they worth?'

'I don't know. My wife gave them to me as gifts ... this one on my left hand twenty years ago when I married her ... and this one on my right hand seventeen years ago when I promised I'd stop going to school.'

With a sardonic smile she muttered, 'You must write down a value!' So I took the forms and wrote down – two rings $200 USD.

I started to open my carry-on bag which I had seen the others ahead of me do. She quickly stamped my forms, handed them to me and waved me through!

'Thank you Lord for answering my prayer,' I whispered. 'And thank you Dianne for these rings!'

God had again accomplished the impossible as he did for each of my five travelling companions.

Our Bibles were for the fast growing church in Vietnam. On Sunday we worshipped with believers in a sanctuary of the Evangelical Church of Vietnam. That was one of two churches in the world I have visited where an unusual announcement was made: 'Do not come next Sunday so others who could not get in today can share in the service.' (The other church was Pastor Lamb's house church in Guangzhou, China.)

The exhortation that morning was 'Be ready to lay down your life for the Lord!' While talking with Pastor Mieng after the service, I asked him what message I could share with Christians in the free world about their situation. He replied, 'Romans 8:36.'

> *'[For your sake we face death all day long; we are considered as sheep to be slaughtered.]*

But we cannot take this verse out of context. The pastor could have responded 'Psalm 44:22' – the Old Testament verse quoted by the Apostle Paul in Romans 8:36.

The preceding verse in Romans eight begins, *'Who shall separate us from the love of Christ?'* The obvious answer is understood to be Satan – the accuser of the saints, our ultimate enemy. The rest of the verse answers a 'what' question with the type of things Satan uses to try to make believers think they are separated from God's love: trouble, hardship, persecution, famine, nakedness, danger or sword.

Trouble or Hardship or Persecution

The Church in Communist Vietnam is a good illustration of how our enemy uses the tactic of persecution. All areas where Western missionaries had worked were severely repressed. Believers were told constantly that they were agents of the CIA. This was especially true in the church in tribal areas. Large city churches were constantly monitored by government informers.

Even as I write there are still restrictions placed on house fellowship pastors and people in the country. And Christian literature is still in short supply.

When Pastor Ha began planting a church in Ho Chi Minh City in the late 70s, it had twenty-nine members. They were permitted to use the sanctuary of the old International Church of Saigon. By the time of his imprisonment in late 1983, they had grown to 5,000 members. Every month they experienced eighty to one hundred conversions. One year they water baptized over eight hundred believers.

They had grown significantly because of three-hour prayer meetings every morning and Bible Studies every evening. It took four services on Sundays to get everyone into the large sanctuary.

Every week government informers were in attendance to see if they could catch him making politically motivated statements in his preaching. One Sunday evening's service there were twelve such men. One got converted and told the pastor about the other eleven.

Just before Christmas in 1983, the police arrived at the time of morning prayer. They confiscated the Bibles and hymn books, closed the church and locked the gate. Many believers stood weeping at the gates for days.[1]

Pastor Ha's family was evicted from their apartment at the back of the church and he was taken away to prison. Earlier you read the results of the continuing spiritual impact they made. They realized that trouble, hardship and persecution could never separate them from the love of Jesus.

Mrs Ha now says that God brought much good out of their hardships. She felt the Lord rewarded her by the decision of her two children to follow the Lord and become well disciplined Christians.

The Church in Vietnam continues to grow in spite of the pressures – especially in home groups – even though several pastors of house fellowships have spent years in prison. One fellowship led 2300 people to Christ in one year. Another is growing at the rate of 300 new believers per month.

Famine or Nakedness

My good friend and former colleague, Terry Madison, now with World Vision, talked with a lady in Saigon whose husband was in one of the country's notoriously horrible re-education camps. She was allowed to visit him twice a year for a half hour each time. But she could only afford to make the trip to the north once a year.

As a sensitive journalist, Terry asked her, 'What do you and your husband talk about in your half hour together?'

With tears coursing down her cheeks she replied, 'We don't talk, we just look at each other and cry!'

Wilson Chen from Vietnam spent five years in one of those harsh and primitive re-education camps. He was forced to spend long hours of hard back-breaking work clearing jungles for farmland, cutting trees for lumber and farming the fields.

He had looked forward to a successful secular career and also to marrying his lovely girlfriend. In his final year in camp, he received the crushing news that his girl friend had given up hope, married another and escaped from Vietnam.

The camp food was barely enough to keep him alive. 'The constant brutality attacked our minds and spirits; the malnutrition attacked our bodies,'[2] he recalls. The constant hunger drove them to eat anything. He would search the ground with other prisoners for rats, toads, worms, snakes, insects and birds to supplement their diet and keep them alive and to simply ease the feeling of constant hunger.

Wilson remembers companions who went insane from the pressure of hunger. Others committed suicide. Many died from diseases caused by the malnutrition.

Every night they were subjected to mental torture and political indoctrination. Always in their minds were thoughts of escape.

But Wilson Chen says, 'It was hope in the Lord Jesus that kept me alive. I fed this hope by secretly reading the Scriptures...'[3] In that camp situation, Wilson promised the Lord that he would serve him if he ever received the opportunity. The Holy Spirit whispered to him, 'You have opportunities right here!' Very soon three fellow-prisoners came to know the Lord.

Camp experiences helped him reflect on the significance of the sufferings of Jesus. In that context he found refreshment and exhilaration in his own weakness. And he says, '...[Jesus gave me] peace in the midst of tribulation.'[4]

At the same time in neighbouring Kampuchea, now Cambodia, Narun Van shares how he was forced to work on a farm by the ruling Khymer Rouge. He worked daily from 5:00 a.m. till 9:00 p.m. There was little food and the work was hard and humiliating. He shares a significant incident:

'Then one day one of the guards who knew I had two copies of the Bible asked me to give him one ... I did not want to give it to him but knew I must. Every day the guard used one page for cigarette paper, but before tearing out the page, he read it front and back.

One day he came to the doorway and we began to talk. He said, "If you will tell me how I can become a Christian I will bring you food." ... A strange kind of friendship developed between us. He kept his word and each night brought us food. I grew stronger and my children improved too. That guard became a Christian.'[5]

Narun Van escaped to Thailand with his wife and four children. Today he pastors in Australia. He says,

'I want to tell all people about the God who loves them and hears and answers prayer. He is the real God.'[6]

Danger or Sword

There are few countries where suffering and death have decimated both the citizenship and the church more than in Cambodia. This land is best known by the docu-drama movie titled 'The Killing Fields'. The Cambodians have a proverb that is a powerful statement of the powerless: **'When the elephants dance, the grass gets trampled!'**

When Pol Pot came to power on April 17th, 1975, a systematic slaughter of the seven million Cambodian people began. As many as one million people were murdered – possibly many more. Hundreds of thousands fled to safety in Thailand.[7]

God allowed some of his children to be murdered – including eleven pastors. He allowed others to escape.

During the Cambodian civil war in the early seventies, I visited the country several times working on Christian broadcast matters for FEBC shortwave transmissions from the Philippines. It was then I became friends with a dynamic national leader named Son Sonne. He worked for the Bible Society in Cambodia and was a lay preacher.

The last time I saw him was in 1974. He was so excited about the great opportunities he had to preach to thousands of refugees flooding into the capital of Phnom Penh. And hundreds at a time were responding to the gospel.

The national church decided Son Sonne should leave the country for leadership training. He could do this in the Philippines where he could also help with the Christian radio ministry beamed back to his country. We prepared a home for him and his wife and their five children on our compound north of Manila. Air tickets were purchased and they were miraculously granted the difficult exit permits needed to leave Cambodia.

The family was to fly to Manila on April 15th, 1975. But on April 14th the International airport at Phnom Penh was bombed by the Khymer Rouge and all commercial flights were cancelled. Three days later the country fell to the communist guerrillas and their campaign of terror.

When I visited Phnom Penh again in 1984, it was a very emotional experience for me. I was told that Son Sonne and family were some of the skeleton bones I saw piled high at the memorial of the Killing Fields near Takmau.

I am anxiously awaiting the opportunity to meet Son Sonne in heaven and learn why God left him in the country. I believe he must have been mightily used of God in the last days of his life.

On the other hand, is the remarkable testimony of Pastor Ung Sophal who had established eight house churches in Phnom Penh and the surrounding provinces.

Shortly before the country fell to the Khymer Rouge in 1975, he was sharing with six hundred Christians gathered at a church meeting. Aware of the danger ahead, they agreed to write their names on the back wall of the church building if they made it back to Phnom Penh. 'Only three names were ever to appear on the wall – that of Ung and two others who narrowly escaped death.'[8]

He and his wife lost their third and youngest child during the genocide. After many close calls, Ung was separated from his wife and children and sent to work in the fields. During these very difficult times, he still was able to lead sixty-five people to

Jesus and even water baptize them. God miraculously spared his life on numerous occasions.

When the Vietnamese invaded Kampuchea – as it was then called – in 1979, Ung Sophal was able to return to Phnom Penh. It was now a ghost town. With a handful of other Christians, he started a house church which grew from five members to six hundred in eight months.

That Christmas he invited some Christians to his home for a fellowship – including some Christian westerners working for aid organizations. Two weeks later he was arrested for this 'illegal' activity and accused of holding a political meeting with CIA participation.

He was interrogated for days and beaten severely. When the interrogation proved profitless, he was left in prison for five months chained hand and foot. He lost seventy-five pounds and was very sick but he heard the Lord instruct him to fast and be silent for three days.

The authorities became alarmed at the end of his fast and took him to the hospital thinking he was dying. There he constantly heard the sounds of other people being tortured with electricity and being beaten and kicked.

'Even without the beatings it was very hard,' he said, 'I had a taste of Hell, but God protected me.' [9]

Ung Sophal was successfully treated by a Cuban doctor who was also a Christian (God has His people everywhere). One night when the electricity went out because of a tropical storm, the doctor helped Ung escape. Later he escaped with his wife and children to Thailand and spent ten years ministering to other Cambodian exiles – the last five years as a widower. Here is how one report about him concludes:

'In 1990, as restrictions against Christianity began to be eased in Cambodia, Ung made his first visit back to his homeland to encourage and teach the church. Word of his return spread quickly and three hundred people came to see him.

Cambodia's Prime Minister also requested to see Ung. During a 40-minute meeting, the pastor shared his vision for rebuilding the ravaged nation, including his plans to establish orphanages, educational facilities and hospitals...

Ung is eager for the task ahead. "I want to build my people," he said. "God has a great work yet to do in Cambodia." [10]

Super-Victors

The context following the Romans 8:36 reference of Vietnamese Pastor Mieng answers the questions asked in verse 35 as an obvious **No!** Rather in all these things thrown at us and through which we may be required to pass, we can be **'more than conquerors!'**

The supreme example for me of the many who are super-victors is a Cambodian Christian whom I will simply call Cham. As a young Christian, he witnessed a Khymer Rouge soldier – a youth he knew from school – bludgeon his mother to death by hitting her repeatedly over the head with a wooden board.

Cham suffered from severe depression over memories of that incident for many months. But eventually the Lord helped him gain victory over it. Ten years later, Cham was walking down the main street of Phnom Penh and saw the young man who had killed his mother. The young man was very fearful of revenge when he recognized Cham approaching him.

With moist eyes Cham looked at him and said, 'In the name of Jesus, I forgive you!' [11]

Oswald Chambers says,

> 'We are super-victors with a joy that comes from experiencing the very things which look as if they are going to overwhelm us. Huge waves that would frighten an ordinary swimmer produce a tremendous thrill for the surfer who has ridden them ... The things we try to avoid and fight against – tribulation, suffering and persecution – are the very things that produce abundant joy in us.' [12]

In the Romans eight passage, the Apostle Paul goes on to say:

'For I am convinced that
neither death nor life,
neither angels nor demons,
neither the present nor the future,
nor any powers,
neither height nor depth,
nor anything else in all creation,
will be able to separate us from the
love of God that is in Christ Jesus
our Lord.' [13]

My strongest visual memory when hearing this scripture read is from the movie about the life of Corrie Ten Boom, *The Hiding Place*. Papa Ten Boom reads this scripture aloud to the family in their home above his watch shop in Haarlem during World War II. Soon after, the hiding place for Jews is discovered and they all experience the horrors of prison and concentration camp – and even death for Papa and Betsie.

Corrie, however, spends the rest of her life travelling the world with one main message: **God's love is much stronger than the deepest darkness**.

One of our brave colleagues visited Pastor Matta Bush when he was in prison in Sudan. The Pastor had served seven years of a thirty year sentence with no visits from his wife and children. He concluded,

'I believe that God has put me here for a reason: to share the Gospel with other prisoners. If I would not be here, who would reach them? Many people, including guards have accepted the Lord. **As for me: I am doing fine because I experience that nothing can separate me from the love of Christ**.' [14] (emphasis added)

Wilson Chen who spent five years in that terrible re-education camp in Vietnam says,

'I could not forget that nothing had separated me from the love of Christ ... And nothing need separate me from

160

the love of Christ in the days ahead ... Looking back, I can see that I experienced God's love more when I was in the concentration camp than at any other time in my life...

... But I pray that the lessons of faith that I learned may now bear fruit, keeping me humble and trusting, as I continue to walk and learn from my Savior.' [15]

Another great example for me of super-victorious Christian living is what I have witnessed on my many trips to the island of Cuba. All of the above negative conditions are prevalent in the Christian Church there. My heart is still heavy as I recall the literal malnutrition among believers seen just months ago. Yet I cannot forget the scene of hungry, humble young people excitedly singing from their hearts the very lively melody of one of my favourite Cuban Christian songs based on Habakkuk 3:17–18:

'Though the fig tree does not bud
and there are no grapes on the vines,
though the olive crop fails
and the fields produce no food,
although there are no sheep in the pen
and no cattle in the stalls,
yet I will rejoice in the Lord,
I will be joyful in God my Saviour.'

This is super-victorious living! We love Him because He first loved us. And **nothing** can ever separate us from His love!

Therefore, live ever aware of God's presence and His love!

Lord, you have promised that nothing can separate me from your love. Forgive me when I take my eyes off you and focus on the strategies of Satan. Help me to walk in your power as a victorious conqueror. And thank you that you alone are worthy of my wholehearted love.

*If you are burning with
the love of Jesus, don't worry:
everyone will know.
They will say,
'I want to get close to this person
who is so full of God.'*

Henry Nouwen

Success is neither fame, wealth nor power: rather it is seeking, knowing, loving and obeying God. If you seek, you will know; if you know, you will love; if you love, you will obey.

Charles Malik

Conclusion

Difficult Assignments

It is possible! The Suffering Church by example proves to us that it is indeed possible to lose everything ... to suffer everything ... to endure everything ... yet maintain a joyful spirit and heart of love for the Lord.

So often our major shortcoming is simply to doubt that we could go through those experiences and come out of them as refined and triumphant as we have witnessed others in these few chapters. Jesus never promised that our life would be easy – just fulfilling. He never promised that things would be fair – only that he would be just.

Though we might think that life is too hard for these brothers and sisters about whom we've been reading, we have been given perhaps an even tougher spiritual assignment. Yet the principles in dealing with it remain the same.

Ruth Graham shares a convicting story about a Christian who had just arrived in a free country from years of persecution. He was appalled at the seeming casual commitment to Jesus and materialistic contamination of these Christians. And he said so.

Some time later he returned to visit the friend to whom he had spoken so bluntly when he first arrived:

'He asked if his friend remembered what he had said, the bitterness of his criticism. The friend remembered.

The man stood silent for a few moments, reflecting. The friend tensed for a second attack.

"I have come to apologize both for what I said and the way in which I said it," he said simply. "I was merely afraid. I did not know how dangerous freedom could be. It has been a year now. And I am worse than those I criticized."

Then he added a significant statement: **"It is more difficult to live the Christian life under freedom than under repression."** [1] (emphasis added)

Iranian Christian leader Luke Yagnazar lives in the United States. He concludes,

'It is more difficult to be a Christian in the USA than in Iran. There you are either a Christian or not!' [2]

Pastor Samuel Lamb in southern China says,

'We have physical persecution but you have materialism. Your lot is harder because we know what we are spiritually fighting. Many times you don't.' [3]

Another Chinese church leader adds,

'Once you are chasing after money there is no time and energy for church affairs ... And the government knows that materialism will destroy the church faster than persecution can ... **I tell my co-workers in China that the biggest enemy we're facing is no longer communism, it's materialism**.' [4] (emphasis added)

A Chinese believer who experienced much suffering for her faith expressed it this way,

'We are constantly reminded that we are in a spiritual warfare. We know whom we are fighting for. We know who the enemy is. And we are fighting. Perhaps we should pray for you Christians outside China. In your leisure, in your affluence, in your freedom, sometimes you no longer realize that you are in a spiritual warfare.' [5]

On arriving in the USA, Mrs Ha from Vietnam shared that she is no longer afraid of suffering and persecution. 'What I fear now,' she adds, 'is that living in freedom will cause coldness and losing the power of the Holy Spirit.' [6]

Ugandan pastor, Kefa Sempangi documents his family escaping death by the narrowest of margins. After studying at an American seminary he states:

'In Uganda, Penina and I read the Bible for hope and life. We read to hear God's promises, to hear his commands and obey them. There had been no time for arguments and no time for religious discrepancies or doubts.

Now, in the security of a new life and with the reality of death fading from mind, I found myself reading Scripture to analyze texts and speculate about meaning. I came to enjoy abstract theological discussions with my fellow students and, while these discussions were intellectually refreshing, it wasn't long before our fellowship revolved around ideas rather than the work of God in our lives...

The biggest change came to my prayer life. In Uganda I had prayed with a deep sense of urgency. I refused to leave my knees until I was certain I had been in the presence of the resurrected Christ ... Now, after a year in Philadelphia, the urgency was gone. When I prayed publicly I was more concerned to be theologically correct than to be in God's presence. Even in private my prayers were no longer the helpless cries of a child. They were spiritual tranquilizers, thoughts that made no contact with anything outside themselves. More and more, I found myself coming to God with vague requests for gifts I did not expect.' [7]

Kefa Sempangi goes on to share how God rebuked him and called him to obedience in using the little he had to bless the Suffering Church in Uganda. The humble beginnings developed into the Africa Foundation, Inc. His now specific prayers became the means by which he came face to face again with the living God. A new and fresh understanding of the Bible came to his heart.

Brother Andrew says,

> 'We don't deserve our freedom; we have it by God's grace for a purpose – to care for and strengthen other members of the Body of Christ who are suffering!'

Many people with whom I discuss these issues conclude that since there seems to be more unity and strength in the church in countries where outside pressure is the norm, we need to pray for persecution to come our way.

But a closer observation of the church in many middle eastern countries and in North Africa reveals that persecution does not guarantee church unity and growth or revival.

On the other hand, freedom or absence of persecution cannot be blamed for our lack of church unity and growth. South Korea is an excellent example of a free country where the church is experiencing significant growth and revival.

In the year 1880, there was not one indigenous church in Korea. Today in South Korea there are over 7,000 churches. Of these, nine are among the largest churches in the world. These churches are known first for their prayer and devotional life and then their missionary zeal.

I believe Romanian pastor Dr Paul Negrut has the most perceptive conclusion. He says,

> **'What makes the difference is how we respond to persecution and how we respond to freedom.'**[8]

He explains that during times of pressure, Christians are forced to seriously grapple with basic questions because they have to be sure their faith is worth dying for.

He reasons that two things are necessary to be a strong disciple of Jesus: spiritual knowledge and spiritual power. Spiritual knowledge is summed up in answers to three significant questions: Who is Jesus? ... What is the Bible? ... What is the church?

Applying this to his own country, he says,

> 'Now those people who came to the conclusion that Christ is God incarnated, that the Bible is the Word of God and that the church is the body of Christ, those people were willing to spend years in jail and even to die. That's the strength of the Romanian church.'[9]

He adds that it is prayer and a moment by moment walk in the Spirit which brings powerful dependence on God when Christians are very much aware that this day may be their last. And when they realize that even the next hour will come and go only by the grace of God.

Dr Negrut thus correctly identifies the essence of spiritual success. And it does not need to be a secret:

> **'It is not persecution itself but the lessons learned under persecution that make and keep the church and an individual believer strong in the Lord ... what makes the difference is how we respond to persecution and how we respond to freedom.** [10]

May we be willing to learn and act accordingly ... and be prepared for the hardest assignments. You too can be a spiritual success! Be strong in the Lord!

> The figure of the crucified invalidates all thought which takes success for its standard.
>
> Dietrich Bonhoeffer

Seven Secrets of Spiritual Success

from the Suffering Church

Secret One – Wholehearted love for God

What our good and loving God wants most from you and me is our undivided love for him – above all else – proven in obedience to him and love for all others . . . and rewarded with his goodness and fatherly caring.

Secret Two – Wholehearted commitment to God

Jesus who gave his all for you and me asks, no he demands, reckless abandonment and wholehearted commitment to the point of death from those who would be his disciples . . . rewarding them with the overcomer's crown.

Secret Three – Wholehearted service for God

Because of Jesus' love and example for us, we prove our love for him as faithful bond servants – wherever we are placed . . . and his reward is his personal presence with us always.

Secret Four – Enjoy the trip

Being in absolute surrender to God and filled with his Spirit to overflowing, we pilgrims can truly be persons of contagious joy . . . regardless of the struggles of this earthly pilgrimage or the pressures of refining persecution . . . and are rewarded by God's protection.

Secret Five – Spiritual strength for the battle

The whole armour of God is needed to stand against the devil's schemes . . . but the Word of God internalized, and Spirit-led prayer will enable the believer to strike offensively . . . and with perseverance remain victorious even under the most difficult attacks.

Secret Six – All in the family

Jesus Christ calls his followers to be the church – not play church. Our passion for him is to be followed by our passion for the family of God. As the church, we are to fulfil the functions of evangelism, discipleship, fellowship and worship.

Secret Seven – The full circle of love

Absolutely nothing can separate us from the love of God that is in Christ Jesus our Lord! Therefore, love him with all your being.

Endnotes

Introduction

1. Authorized version of the Bible.
2. Oswald Chambers, *My Utmost For His Highest* (Grand Rapids, MI: Discovery House Publishers, 1992) page for June 3.

Chapter 1

1. At that time approximately equal to a US Dollar.
2. Richard J. Foster and James Bryan Smith, *Devotional Classics* (San Francisco, CA: Harper Collins, 1990), p. 31.
3. Matthew 22:37–40.
4. Numbers 14:24. It is interesting to note that Caleb accepted Joshua's later appointment as leader to succeed Moses.
5. Revelation 3:16.
6. Carl Lawrence, *The Church in China* (Minneapolis, MN: Bethany House Publishers, 1985), p. 44.
7. John 15:15.
8. Oswald Chambers, *My Utmost For His Highest* (Westwood, NJ: Dodd Mead & Co. Inc.), pp. 118 and 194.
9. Bernard Bangley, modern readings of Thomas à Kempis, *The Imitation of Christ* (UK: Highland), p. 33.
10. Mikail Khorev, *Letters From a Soviet Prison Camp* (Eastbourne, UK: Monarch Publications Ltd, 1986), pp. 89–90.
11. *Ibid.*, p. 147.
12. From cassette recording of message given in Holland in April 1990.
13. Brother David with Lela Gilbert, *Walking The Hard Road* (London, UK: Marshall Pickering, 1989), pp. 39–41.

14. Judith Wark, *News Network International*, News Service December 21, 1993, p. 60.
15. Paul Estabrooks, unpublished manuscript *Songs of Deliverance*, transcription from cassettes of autobiography of Mrs Chen in China.
16. Luke 18:29–30.
17. Terry Brand, 'God's Love Overcomes', *Open Doors Newsbrief*, July–August 1990, p. 3.
18. Charles Colson, *Loving God* (Grand Rapids, MI: Zondervan Publishing House, 1983), p. 172.
19. John 14:15.
20. Personal interview in Hong Kong, May 1980.
21. 'Inside Castro's Prisons', *TIME*, August 15, 1983, p. 20.
22. Armando Valladares, *Against All Hope* (New York: Alfred A. Knopf, 1986), p. 199.
23. F. Kefa Sempangi with Barbara R. Thompson, *A Distant Grief* (Glendale, CA: Regal Books, 1979), pp. 161 and 188.
24. Jan Pit, *Bound To Be Free: With The Suffering Church* (Tonbridge, Kent, UK: Sovereign World, 1995) p. 86.
25. From English translation of letter originally in Farsi.
26. Margaret Fishback Powers, *Footprints* (Toronto, Canada: HarperCollins, 1993) p. 9.

Chapter 2

1. English translation from original Vietnamese letter dated July 5, 1986.
2. Canada's Registered Retirement Savings Plan (usually invested in Mutual Funds).
3. Jim Cunningham, 1994.
4. Luke 9:23.
5. The word 'disciple' is the most common term used to describe Jesus' followers in the New Testament. It occurs 269 times while the word 'Christian' is found only three times.
6. From cassette recorded message, Missionsfest, Vancouver, Canada, January 1992.
7. 2 Samuel 24:24.
8. Acts 20:24.
9. 'How Much Did It Cost?' *FEBC SIGNAL*, Vol. 21 No. 4, April 1979, p. 1.
10. Luke 14:33.
11. Oswald Chambers, p. 1.

12. Oswald Chambers, pp. 55 and 165.
13. David Y.P. Wang, *8 Lessons We Can Learn From The Church In China* (Hong Kong: Asian Outreach Publication) pp. 5–7.
14. 'How Much Did It Cost?', *FEBC SIGNAL*, Vol. 21 No. 4, April 1979, p. 1.
15. George Middleton, Orillia, Canada, Sudan report newsletter, p. 2.
16. John 12:24.
17. Dietrich Bonhoeffer, *The Cost of Discipleship* (New York: Macmillan Publishing Company, 1949), p. 7.
18. *Dateline*, A Publication of Arab World Ministries, Cambridge ON, Canada, January 1991, p. 2.
19. The story of this dear pastor and his well-known house church is told in the very readable book, *Bold As A Lamb* (Zondervan), written by Ken Anderson.
20. J. Lee Grady, 'Trial By Fire In Havana', *Charisma*, January, 1994, p. 80.
21. Thomas C. Oden, 'The Church Castro Couldn't Kill', *Christianity Today*, April 25, 1994, p. 19.
22. *Ibid.*, p. 22.
23. Jamie Buckingham, Best Quotes', *Charisma*, August 1995, p. 51.
24. Matthew 8:20.
25. *12,000 Quotes*, p. 300.
26. Christopher Young, 'The Tiananmen File', *The Toronto Star*, Saturday, June 2, 1990, p. D-1.
27. Emily Mitchell, 'All Eyes on the Storm', *TIME*, October 23, 1995, p. 77.
28. Patrick Martin, 'Death Holds No Fear For Muslim Militants', *The Globe and Mail*, Friday, May 12, 1995. p. A-10.
29. George Otis, Jr, *The Last of the Giants* (Tarrytown, NY: Fleming H. Revell Company, 1991), p. 261.
30. David B. Barrett, 'Annual Statistical Table on Global Mission: 1996', *International Bulletin of Missionary Research*, Vol. 20, No. 1, January 1996, p. 25.
31. 'Martyrdom: The Most Potent Factor In World Evangelization', *Asian Report*, Report 191, Vol. 24, No. 5, Sept–Dec. 1991, p. 5.
32. Dan Wooding, '330,000 believers are martyred annually, reports researcher David Barrett', *Christian News*, July 19, 1987, p. 17.
33. *Op. cit.*, p. 5.
34. Myrna Grant, *Letters To Graduates* (Nashville, TN: Abingdon Press, 1990), p. 17.
35. Dick Eastman, 'A Martyr's Measure of Commitment', *Every Home For Christ*, June 1993, p. 3.

36. 'Iranian Minister Executed by Authorities', *The Church Around The World*, March 1991.
37. English translation from letter originally in Farsi.
38. Barbara Baker, *News Network International*, News Service January 21, 1994. p. 5.
39. 'Answered Prayers', *TIME*, January 31, 1994, p. 9.
40. Isaiah 57:1–2.
41. 'Reign of terror strikes Iran's Christians', *Open Doors with Brother Andrew Newsbrief*, Vol. 9, Issue 9, September, 1994, pp. 1–2.
42. Danyun, *Lilies Amongst Thorns* (Tonbridge, Kent, UK: Sovereign World, 1991) p. 30.
43. 'The Last Days of Watchman Nee', *Overseas Missionary Fellowship Pray For China Fellowship*, April, 1993, p. 2.
44. *Ibid.*, p. 7.
45. Anil Stephen, 'Paul Negrut's Vision For Romania', *News Network International*, News Service September 23, 1992, p. 54.
46. Joseph Tson, 'Thank You For The Beating', Reprinted from *Christian Herald*, April, 1988, pp. 3–4.
47. Jan Pit, *Persecution: It Will Never Happen Here?* (Orange, CA: Open Doors With Brother Andrew Inc., 1981) pp. 118–119.

Chapter 3

1. Personal report from Reg Reimer from translation of letter from Vietnam, 1985.
2. Cornerstone Ministries International letter, April 19, 1993.
3. Jonathan Goforth, 'The Story of Zia Nodrat', Toronto, Canada: Fellowship of Faith.
4. Paul Negrut, from cassette recording of message given in Holland, April, 1990.
5. Danyun, *Lilies Amongst Thorns* (Tonbridge, Kent, UK: Sovereign World Ltd, 1991), pp. 202–203.
6. Exodus 21:6.
7. Brother Andrew, 'Thinking About You', *Personally Yours* (UK: Open Doors with Brother Andrew, 1995) p. 11.
8. Ho Hieu Ha, from message at Open Doors Prayer Conference, October, 1991.
9. Cuong Nguyen, from message given at Open Doors Prayer Conference, October 1992.
10. Jim Reapsome, 'Chains and Hershey's Kisses', *World Pulse*, Vol. 28 No. 18, September 24, 1993 p. 9.

11. Carl Lawrence, *The Church in China* (Minneapolis, MN: Bethany House Publishers, 1985), p. 149.
12. Philippians 1:14.
13. 'Ethiopian Believers Continue Witness Despite Imprisonment', *Decision*, December 1987, p. 19.
14. 'Prisoners Released', *Christianity Today*, May 12, 1989, p. 58.
15. Armando Valladares, *Against All Hope* (New York: Alfred A. Knopf, 1986) p. 199.
16. Carl Lawrence, pp. 44–45.
17. Open Doors Interview, June 1993.
18. Open Doors Report, November, 1993.
19. Ross Paterson, *Heartcry For China* (Chichester, UK: Sovereign World Ltd, 1989) p. 186.
20. Open Doors Report, December 1987.
21. 'Sons of God', *Asian Report*, p. 17.
22. Myrna Grant, *Vanya* (Alamonte Springs, Florida: Creation House, 1974), p. 137.
23. Thomas C. Oden, 'The Church Castro Couldn't Kill', *Christianity Today*, April 25, 1994, p. 22.
24. Carl Lawrence, *Glasnost and the Believers in the Soviet Union* (Hollywood, CA: Haven of Rest Ministries, 1988), p. 18.
25. *Ibid.*, pp. 24–25.
26. *Ibid.*, p. 25.
27. Gul Masih, translation of letter written in Urdu from Sargodha Jail, March 8, 1993.
28. Oswaldo Magdandal, *Arrested In The Kingdom* (Witney, Oxon, UK: Open Doors UK, 1993), p. 22.
29. Dennis Balcombe, 'A Heroine Of Faith Risks Death In China', *Charisma*, January, 1994 p. 33.
30. Open Doors Interview, January, 1994.
31. Peter de Bruijne, *Siberian Miracle* (London, UK: Marshall Pickering, 1990), pp. 175–176.
32. Lois Olson, recorded in prayer letter from Florence Olson, March 1994.

Chapter 4

1. *Asian Development Brief* (Hong Kong: Open Doors, No. 32, October–November 1992) p. 2.
2. Psalm 13:1 and Psalm 89:46.
3. Psalm 80:4.
4. Psalm 82:2.

5. Revelation 6:11.
6. Acts 1:18a.
7. Psalm 90:12.
8. Joni Earickson Tada, message at Vancouver, Missionsfest February 13, 1994.
9. Mikail Khorev, *Letters From a Soviet Prison Camp* (Eastbourne, UK: Monarch Publications, 1986), p. 190.
10. Oswald Chambers, *My Utmost For His Highest* (Westwood, NJ: Dodd Mead & Company, 1935) p. 39.
11. F.W. Boreham, 'Abraham Lincoln's Text', *Just Thinking*, Winter 1993, p. 6.
12. Stephen Olford, message at National Religious Broadcasters Convention, Los Angeles, February, 1993.
13. Malcolm Muggeridge, *The End of Christendom*, quoted by Ravi Zacharius in 'Reflections on Elections', *Just Thinking*, Winter 1993, p. 3.
14. John 17:14–18.
15. Gordon Fee, message at Vancouver Missionsfest, January 31, 1993.
16. Carl Lawrence, *The Church in China* (Minneapolis MN: Bethany House Publishers, 1985), p. 144.
17. F. Kefa Sempangi, *A Distant Grief* (Glendale, Ca: Regal Books, 1979), p. 11.
18. Colossians 1:24.
19. Acts 16.
20. Ivan Antonov, 'Survival 101: How to prepare for imprisonment', *Prisoner Bulletin*, 1989, p. 13.
21. *Asian Report, Asian Outreach*, pp. 17–18.
22. Tony Lambert, *The Resurrection of the Chinese Church* (London: Hodder & Stoughton, 1991), p. 179.
23. Bill Harding IV, 'Hearing the Songs of Praise in Ethiopia', *Decision*, November 1991, p. 18.
24. From personal interview with Alexander, June 1989.
25. 'The Lord Knows', *China and the Church Today*, Vol. 7:3 June 1985, p. 7.
26. Dorothy Ai Chung, 'How God Taught Me Brokenness', *Christian Aid*, Charlottesville, VA.
27. Dale McClain, 'Schooled In Suffering', *OMS Outreach*, January/March 1992, p. 7.
28. Erwin Lutzer, *Where Do We go From Here?* pp. 43–44.
29. Hebrews 10:34.
30. Keith Price, *Frontline Christian*, Aug/Sept 1992, p. 6.

31. Cornelius Plantinga, Jr, 'Hard Assignments', *Christianity Today*, June 20, 1994, p. 42.
32. CCRC, May/June, 1985.
33. Tony Lambert, p. 164.
34. Open Doors interview on cassette, UK, 1993.
35. Andrew Wark, 'Vietnam At The Crossroads', *News Network International*, Special Report, February 23, 1994, p. 4.
36. David Porter, *Bamboo in Winter* (London: Marshall Pickering, 1992), p. 97.
37. Timothy Wang and Doug Wicks, 'A Citizen Without Rights', *Alliance Witness*, January 15, 1986, p. 11.
38. Oswald Chambers, p. 39.
39. Mikhail Khorev, p. 101.
40. Poem by George Matheson.
41. J. Christy Wilson, *More to be Desired than Gold* (South Hamilton, MA: Gordon-Conwell Theological Seminary, 1992), p. 172.
42. Open Doors' Islam Development Brief, Vol. No. 30, September 1994, pp. 8–9.
43. 'Apocalypse in Rwanda', *Open Doors with Brother Andrew Newsbrief*, Vol. 9 Issue 10, October, 1994, pp. 2–3.
44. *Ibid.*, p. 3.

Chapter 5

1. Georgi Vins, *Let the Waters Roar: Evangelists In The Gulag* (Grand Rapids, MI: Baker Book House, 1989), p. 163.
2. Ephesians 6:17–19.
3. Dale McClain, 'Schooled In Suffering', *OMS Outreach*, January/March 1992, p. 7.
4. Ivan Antonov, 'Survival 101: How to prepare for imprisonment' *Prisoner Bulletin*, 1989, p. 13.
5. Georgi Vins, p. 102.
6. Paul Estabrooks, unpublished manuscript, *Songs of Deliverance*, from cassette recorded testimonies of Mrs Chen from China.
7. F. Kefa Sempangi, *A Distant Grief* (Glendale, CA: Regal Books, 1979), pp. 43–44.
8. C. Peter Wagner, 'Our Weapons of Spiritual Warfare', *Asian Report*, Report 197, Vol. 26 No. 5, October/November 1992, p. 2.
9. Ho Hieu Ha, cassette recorded message at Open Doors Prayer Conference, October 1991.
10. Cuong Nguyen, cassette recording of message at Open Doors Prayer Conference, October 1992.

11. Irina Tarushinskaya, *Grey Is The Colour Of Hope* (London: Hodder & Stoughton, 1988).
12. Dick Rodgers, *Irina* (Keston College, UK: Lion Publishing, 1987), p. 175.
13. Open Doors personal interview in Iran.
14. Peter de Bruijne, *Siberian Miracle* (London: Marshall Pickering, 1990), p. 118.
15. Ross Paterson, *Heart Cry For China* (Chichester, UK: Sovereign World, 1989), p. 190.
16. David Wang, 'And They Continued Steadfastly...', *How The Chinese Christians Pray* (Hong Kong: Asian Outreach Publication, 1993), p. 5.
17. Bill Harding IV, 'Hearing The Songs of Praise in Ethiopia', *Decision*, November 1991, p. 18.
18. David Wang, cassette recorded message at Vancouver, Missionsfest, February, 1995.
19. Ross Paterson, p. 193.
20. Personal interview, June, 1992.
21. Oswald Chambers, *My Utmost For His Highest* (Grand Rapids MI: Discovery House, 1992), page for February 22.
22. Dorothy Ai Chang, 'How God Taught Me Brokenness', Christian Aid Brochure.
23. *Voice*, TWR Hong Kong, No. 50, 1993, p. 6.

Chapter 6

1. *More Than Conquerors* (Open Doors With Brother Andrew, 1979), p. 1.
2. *Ibid.*, p. 5.
3. *Ibid.*, p. 6.
4. 'Gold-Edged Bible, With a Zipper', *Open Doors with Brother Andrew Newsbrief*, Vol. 3, Issue 3, March 1988, pp. 1–2.
5. Tony Lambert, *The Resurrection of the Chinese Church*, (London: Hodder & Stoughton, 1991), p. 6.
6. David Wang, 'Witnessing – Nothing Can Stop Us!', *Decision*, October 1992, p. 12.
7. See Matthew 24:14.
8. Tony Lambert, p. 269.
9. Karen M. Feaver, 'Chinese Lessons', *Christianity Today*, May 16, 1994, p. 34.
10. F. Kefa Sempangi with Barbara R. Thompson, *A Distant Grief* (Glendale, CA: Regal Books, 1979), p. 44.

11. Disciple means a learner.
12. Peter de Bruijne, *Siberian Miracle* (London: Marshall Pickering, 1990), p. 105.
13. Oswaldo Magdangal, *Arrested in the Kingdom* (Witney, Oxon, UK: Open Doors UK, 1993), p. 8.
14. Paul Watson, 'Christians in Somalia must worship in secret', *The Toronto Star*, Dec. 24, 1993 p. A16.
15. *Victory In The Battle*, Open Doors With Brother Andrew Seminar, p. IV–3.
16. Charles R. Swindoll, 'Strengthening Your Grip on Encouragement', *New Wine*, May 1984, p. 24.
17. Charles R. Swindoll, *Strengthening Your Grip* (Waco, TX: Word Books, 1982), p. 48.
18. Georgi Vins, *Let The Waters Roar* (Grand Rapids, MI: Baker Book House, 1989), p. 42.
19. Brian Ross, 'Toward An Intimate Fellowship', *Faith Alive*, p. 70.
20. F. Kefa Sempangi, p. 43.
21. Jan Pit, *Persecution: It Will Never Happen Here?* (Santa Ana, CA: Open Doors with Brother Andrew, 1981), p. 73.
22. Translation of hand-written letter in Chinese.
23. David Y.P. Wang, *8 Lessons We Can Learn From The Church In China* (Hong Kong: Asian Outreach International Ltd), pp. 15–16.
24. James I. Packer in the foreword of David F. Wells, *God the Evangelist* (Eerdmans Publishers, 1987), p. xiii.
25. Teresa of Avila, 1515–1582. Original source unknown.

Chapter 7

1. 'Vietnamese Church Closed', *The Alliance Witness*, March 14, 1984, pp. 18–19.
2. Wilson Chen, 'I Learned the Hard Way, But I Learned', *Christianity Today*, March 19, 1982, p. 23.
3. *Ibid.*, p. 23.
4. *Ibid.*, p. 24.
5. Narun Van, 'Arrested in Kampuchea', private report.
6. *Ibid.*
7. Read the book by Carl Lawrence, *The Prince Still Smiled* (Wheaton, IL: Tyndale House, 1979).
8. Andrew Wark, 'After the Killing Fields', *Asian Report*, No. 196 Report 4, Vol. 25, 1992, p. 16.

9. 'Cambodian Tells of Brutality, Torture in Prison Run by Vietnamese', *Los Angeles Times*, Friday, May 15, 1981, p. 7.
10. Andrew Wark, p. 18.
11. Report from Maurice Bauhahn in Singapore, 1984.
12. Oswald Chambers, *My Utmost For His Highest* (Grand Rapids, MI: Discovery House, 1992), page for March 7.
13. Romans 8:38–39.
14. Open Doors Report, June 16, 1993.
15. Wilson Chen, p. 24.

Conclusion

1. Ruth Bell Graham, 'Dangerous Freedom', *Legacy of a Pack Rat* (Nashville, TN: Thomas Nelson Publishers, 1989), p. 194.
2. Message given at Open Doors Prayer Conference, Costa Mesa, CA, October, 1992.
3. Personal interview, June, 1992.
4. Elizabeth Farrell, 'China – 'Money Madness' Makes Inroads In Church', *News Network International*, News Service August 27, 1993, p. 22.
5. David Y.P. Wang, *8 Lessons We Can Learn From The Church In China* (Hong Kong: Asian Outreach International Ltd.) p. 29.
6. Personal interview, October, 1991.
7. F. Kefa Sempangi with Barbara R. Thompson, *A Distant Grief* (Glendale, CA: Regal Books, 1979), p. 179.
8. Audrey Dorsch, 'After the persecution – what then?', *Faith Today*, November/December 1992, p. 60.
9. *Ibid.*, p. 60.
10. *Ibid.*, p. 60.

Open Doors International Vision Statement

We believe that all doors are open and that God enables his body to go into all the world and preach the gospel. We therefore define our ministry as follows:

- *To strengthen the body of Christ living under restriction or persecution by providing and delivering Bibles, materials, training and other helps, and encouraging it to become involved in world evangelism.*

- *To train and encourage the body of Christ in threatened or unstable areas, to prepare believers to face persecution and suffering, and to equip them to maintain a witness to the gospel of Christ.*

- *To motivate, mobilize, and educate the church in the free world to identify with and become more involved in assisting the suffering church, believing that when 'one member suffers, all the members suffer with it'* (1 Corinthians 12:26 NKJV).

How You and Your Church Can Make a Difference

Prayer – The believers in persecuted lands live in a fierce spiritual battlefield. They need focused, intercessory prayer. Open Doors will send specially prepared prayer information to all those interested in praying for these dear brothers and sisters.

Bible Couriers – For decades Open Doors has been helping believers carry Bibles and Bible study aids into the areas of greatest persecution. God uses ordinary people to take his Word to people living where faith costs the most. You can be one of them.

Adult and Children's Bibles – Many persecuted believers have been beaten and imprisoned for their faith, yet don't have a Bible of their own. The young people in persecuted lands are special targets for false teaching and government control. Leaders know that they must have control of the minds of the youth if they are to stop the spread of Christianity. Open Doors is providing the church with special adult and children's Bibles that present the truth through words and pictures. Your generous gifts make this possible.

Leader Training for Church Growth and Evangelism – Most church leaders in persecuted lands have never had any formal training. Seminaries either don't exist or have been destroyed. Open Doors provides special leader training tailored to the needs and culture of each area. You can help sponsor the training and Christian library materials for one or more brave leaders.

For more information, write:

Open Doors
PO Box 53
Seaforth
New South Wales 2092
Australia

Open Doors
PO Box 597
Streetsville
Ontario L5M 2C1
Canada

Portas Abertas
CP 45 371
CEP 04010-970
São Paulo
Brazil

Portes Ouvertes
BP 5
F-67036 Strasburg
Cédex
France

Porte Aperte
CP 45
37063 Isola della Scala
Verona
Italy

Open Doors
PO Box 47
3850 AA Ermelo
The Netherlands

Open Doors
Box 6123
Auckland 1036
New Zealand

Åpne Dorer
PO Box 4698 Grim
4602 Kristiansand
Norway

Open Doors
PO Box 1573–1155
QCCPO Main
1100 Quezon City
Philippines

Open Doors
1 Sophia Road
06–11 Peace Centre
Singapore 228149

Geopende Deure
Box 990099
Kibler Park 2053
Johannesburg
South Africa

Open Doors
Shehwa Officetel 406
Karakdong 79–4
Songpa-Gu
Seoul 138–160
South Korea

Portes Ouvertes
Case Postale 267
CH-1008 Prilly
Lausanne
Switzerland

Open Doors
PO Box 6
Witney
Oxon OX8 7SP
United Kingdom

Open Doors
PO Box 27001
Santa Ana, CA 92799
USA

If you have enjoyed this book and would like to help us to send a copy of it and many other titles to needy pastors in the **Third World**, please write for further information or send your gift to:

Sovereign World Trust
PO Box 777, Tonbridge
Kent TN11 9XT
United Kingdom

or to the **'Sovereign World'** distributor in your country.

If sending money from outside the United Kingdom, please send an International Money Order or Foreign Bank Draft in STERLING, drawn on a **UK** bank to **Sovereign World Trust**.